The MAGGIE LETTERS

COPING WITH ALZHEIMER'S DISEASE
THROUGH THE RESOURCES OF
THE HUMAN SPIRIT, FAMILY AND SCIENCE

By FELIX J. ROGERS, D.O.

*This book is dedicated to everyone who has re-directed
their life to be present in the care of a
family member or friend who has a chronic illness.
You are doing the right thing.*

Published by the author, Felix J. Rogers, DO in Pleasant Ridge, Michigan

New Blue Publishing

Printer: Sheridan Books

Printed in the United States of America

Book and cover design by Eric Keller

Production by Arlene Cohn

Author photograph by Maureen Dunphy

Set in Whitman, Albertan Pro and Benton

Rogers, Felix J

The Maggie Letters. Coping with Alzheimer's Disease Through the Resources of the Human Spirit, Family and Science

ISBN- 13: 978-0-578-51451-2

Contents

Preface

THIS DISCIPLINE OF WRITING A BOOK brought so much richness to my life. If you are like me, you may spend much of the time thinking about future things or recalling past events. I'm actually just daydreaming most of the time. The past and future wander in and out of my thoughts. I have learned that to write about things of everyday life calls for a sustained effort to maintain an observant mind. The great gift is that this makes ordinary events much more vivid.

Ever since I was 14 years old, I have been advised to keep a journal. I started one in 1961, the year our entire family embarked on a trip around the world. It seems incongruous to say the trip was a life-changing experience since I was barely a teenager, but my diary does capture so much of my excitement and sense of wonder. I learned an important lesson from that initial experience with writing. I fell a few days behind in my journal entries when we were in Malaysia. I felt I needed to catch up before I could return to contemporaneous entries. I now recognize that as a recipe for failure. If I'm going to write, I just need to do it, wherever I am, physically and psychologically. I have to take things as they are. If I'm a week behind in a journal, I now know to pick up with today's entry. If there is an important event that was missed, it can be addressed later. Something like this happened several times in this book, when the press of my professional activities or family demands caused me to fall behind in my writing.

While I am convinced of the many benefits of keeping a journal, I've learned that writing for a public audience is a completely different task. First of all, what makes me think that my experiences are worth telling others about? And, that I have the skills to do so? Secondly, writing a book involves much more consistency than I have previously shown. I've enjoyed the luxury of writing in my journal when I felt like it; long gaps appear between my entries. Further, since they are private, lapses in grammar, punctuation and logic may all be left behind without a second thought.

When I made the decision to explore converting a series of blog posts into a book, I had the happy experience to discover that writing and publishing is an entire world onto its own. My entry into the field was harrowing. I felt like a kid at a junior high school dance, painfully shy and lacking self-confidence. At a silent auction to raise funds for the Rackham Choir in suburban Detroit, Wendy Keebler offered her writing services at an opening bid that was too good to pass up. She read through my draft and gave such supportive comments that I was affirmed in my decision to be a writer.

This world of writing shares some things with medicine. First of all, it can be very opaque to the outsider; the Internet may be as misleading as it is helpful. And, so much of it takes place by collaboration with individuals who never meet, because so much of this is done online. Jennifer Riemenschneider handled all the printing arrangements for Sheridan Press. Jennifer John proofread the entire manuscript and offered editing suggestions. Arlene Cohn handled production and layout. I never met any of them. My only interaction was to speak with Jennifer John by telephone. Each of them was talented, efficient with their time and mine, and invisible.

Eric Keller designed the book, including the cover, font selection and general layout. Eric also coordinated the book production, arranging the expert collaborators mentioned above. It was a pleasant surprise to learn that he lives in my neighborhood. In fact, he has strolled past my house many times, walking his two dogs. Eric is a dog-lover extraordinaire. Putting it informally, he has two mixed breed dogs. Jake is trained as a therapy dog and Kaya is the opposite: nervous, shy and sound sensitive. Eric enjoys two days a week with Jake at two major hospitals and an elementary school here in the metropolitan Detroit area. He is the author of "Dogs I Have Known," a hilarious collection of hand-drawn portraits of 29 dogs who may have been artists, poets and philosophers; their insights have been inferred by the author, who channels these likeable canines, dressed as they are in business suits, smart hats and stylish scarves. Their thoughts devolve into pithy observations on the human condition and life in general.

Eric and I spent a couple months of Monday afternoons putting this book together. He is kind and thoughtful, with a pleasantly quirky sense of humor. More to the point, he has the patience to deal with my nascent skills with the computer and my uncanny ability to introduce problems into a manuscript when things were actually going pretty well. He lives on another level than I do. While I am perfectly content with the font selection I get with the Word program on my laptop, Eric subscribes to a service that provides over 1500 font choices. He won't even think about fonts until the book cover is designed.

The satisfaction I have derived from writing this book can be attributed to my writing coach, Maureen Dunphy. She is an accomplished writer herself and leads several writing workshops throughout the year. I was lucky to be able to sign up for private lessons. Before I met with her at a restaurant for breakfast, I got an anonymous text message: "I'm sitting in the back. I'm dressed completely in black." In this era of unsolicited advertisements, I misinterpreted the origin of this message and a long abandoned part of my brain began to race away. Later I figured out that she had my phone number, but she was anonymous to me. That event was as close as we ever got to an element of mystery. In fact, her gift is to dispel obscurity and reveal the essential elements of the narrative thread. She must also have an advanced degree in dealing with cardiologists of advanced age who still act like insecure teenagers. I don't know how many times she tried to explain the passive voice. She grew accustomed to seeing a blank look on my face and would gently move the conversation to the next topic. To her credit, I never once heard her say, "He doesn't get it."

I'm guessing Maureen is about my age, based on the ages of her kids and her parents, but she seems to have a lot more energy than I do. We typically met at 8:00 a.m., after her hour-long swimming work out. The rest of her week might involve several writing classes before she launched out on a book signing tour of 6 cities in 4 days. Whereas many people derive pleasure from a massage, pedicure or manicure, my one-on-one time with Maureen was the ultimate in private indulgence. I can't think of anything more expansive or enjoyable than sitting with my writing coach and working on the lesson at hand. It was much more satisfying than the music lessons I studied throughout high school. Maybe this also is part of the observation that "it is too bad youth is wasted on young people."

Maureen took me through every aspect of preparing a book for publication, including the arduous process of the book proposal, which ended up at about 150 pages. At least 20 book agents looked at various snippets of the proposal without finding anything to convince them to take the bait. Maureen then suggested that I have some energetic and accomplished writers read through The Maggie Letters and offer specific advice and commentary. Mary Robertson, Harah Frost and Theresa Nielsen each took a copy of the manuscript to read it thoughtfully and critically. They found abundant typos, but more importantly gave me solid advice about ways to reform the text, and pointed out areas where my writing seemed obscure. I'm deeply grateful for their insight, and hope I have done justice to their commentary.

My professional background is medicine, so science is my usual frame of reference. With medical writing it was often sufficient to assemble facts and present them in a logical order; craftsmanship could be secondary. I consider poetry, fiction, mystery or adventure to be genre so demanding in terms of writing skills that I would never consider tackling them. I think I chose the easiest format: memoir. The best part of that is I would not need to make anything up, or concoct a plot line, conceal a murderer or anything else. All I needed to do was pay attention to the events at hand. When that triggered a memory, then that gave me more material for writing. If the event touched on information I had from the field of medicine or science, I added that to the mix. If it intersected with an aspect of my personal journey or my contemplative reading, that got stirred in as well.

I consider it inevitable that you the reader will often be at a different point in your life journey. When you come to spots where the events don't "speak to your condition," I trust you will just move on to the next entry. I hope there are more areas of contact than there are misses. After all, I'm doing something pretty basic and universal here – telling a story about my mother and how all of us in the family needed to pull together, summon our personal resources and draw on the gifts of science and the spiritual journey. In the end, all my family and I hoped to do was to implement the life lessons that our parents gave to us, in order to deal with their own medical and personal issues.

Introduction

I BARELY KNEW MY MATERNAL GRANDMOTHER. I was 10 years old when she died of dementia at age 78. My mother called it "senility," and she lived with the recurring fear that this would be her fate as well.[1] When my mother was in her mid-80s, one by one, the members of her immediate family individually recognized that she was slipping into the realm of "cognitive impairment," the polite term used before dementia overtly establishes its irreversible grip.

This book tells of my family's response as our matriarch gradually manifested and then became completely disabled by Alzheimer's disease. In one sense, the situation had a unifying effect on family dynamics, but much of the time it was also quite challenging, involving elements of conflict and drama. Above all, it was emotionally, financially and physically exhausting. Our backgrounds in the healthcare fields were a great benefit, since my brother and I are both cardiologists, one of my sisters is a neurologist, and the other is a psychologist. In addition, we took advantage of the growing literature that supports home-based care for Alzheimer's disease patients.

During this time, as I came to understand a great deal about the neurobiological basis of Alzheimer's disease, I also learned a more important lesson: Loss of cognitive function is a fact of life for a large and growing segment of our society. Dementia itself is a heterogeneous disease, with multiple causes, including Alzheimer's disease, Lewy body dementia and dementia due to vascular disease (multi-infarct dementia). The severity and clinical course of these conditions vary considerably within groups and between patients.

Caring for someone suffering from dementia presents bewildering situations and is enormously frustrating. Many times we wished we had a healthcare navigator to assist us in treatment decisions. Fortunately, we were not entirely alone. Multiple educational and healthcare resources are available for families who find themselves in our situation. This book describes many of the tools that we used to cope with my mother's worsening disease in an effective and loving manner.

The series of "letters" presented in the following pages began in December 2009 when my mother — legally Sheila McGown Rogers, but herein referred to by her family nickname, Maggie — fell and broke her arm. Written as brief email messages, they were intended to keep my family up to date on her status and, with my siblings' responses, to provide a clearinghouse for comments on how all of us, her four children, would assist in her care as her health problems continued. After the initial series of email messages, I discontinued the letters for a period of 10 months, as my mother's first health crisis passed, and life returned to its usual, normal pace.

Soon after my last email letter in late 2009, Maggie was discharged from the hospital to her home in Grosse Ile, Michigan, an island community in the Detroit River attached to the mainland by bridge. She had an uneventful recovery from her elbow fracture while we children tried to pull together to help my parents with their needs at their house. We certainly had the resources to do it well. My older brother, Jody, (so nicknamed to distinguish him from our father, Joseph, whom he was named after) practiced cardiology with me (and with my Dad until he retired) and lived two doors down from our parents. My sister Sheila was trained as a psychologist and, as she was retired, made the decision to move back to Grosse Ile, finding a house a couple of miles from our parents. My house is north of Detroit, 45 minutes away, but I could easily stop by on my way home from my office, a 20-minute drive. Lisa, the youngest sibling, lives in Cleveland. She makes up for the long distance by offering her expertise as a neurologist. While she is a specialist in brain tumors, she knows the field well enough to have helped guide us in Maggie's care.

My father had begun practice as an internist in 1945, and he continued working until May 2012, when he retired at age 91. The emphasis in all his practice was preventive care and environmental medicine. A central feature of the practice was the infusion clinic. Patients were tested for deficiency and for excess. Those with a lack of certain micronutrients received them by IV infusion, and those with heavy metal intoxication had chelation therapy to remove lead, mercury and other metals. In his later years, he limited his practice to a few cardiology patients each day and to his infusion clinic.

After Maggie's fall in 2009, Dad took on the task of caring for her, in addition to continuing his work in the office. As in most other areas outside of medicine, Dad's care for Maggie was self-taught. His instinct was that patients with cognitive decline would benefit from a structured routine. He would arise early every day. With the help of his part-time caregiver, they would rouse Maggie from bed against her mighty objections each day around 8 a.m. Together they helped her dress in appropriate business attire, have a hearty breakfast and put on lipstick. He then drove her to the office and had her join him in meeting with patients. Most days, she also received an intravenous infusion of multi-vitamins and minerals. While she was at the office, she chattered away with the nurses and other patients. Everyone found my folks to be charming, arriving as they did holding hands and greeting everyone fondly, as if they were arriving at a church tea, not a doctor's office.

When office hours ended, about 1 p.m., Maggie and Dad headed home for lunch. Maggie took a long afternoon nap while Dad worked on his patient charts, organized a few things around the house and then turned his attention to dinner. For decades, he had taken advantage of my mother's fabulous cooking ability. In her words, "he recently discovered there was a kitchen in the house." What he lacked in creativity or culinary skills, he attempted to overcome by sheer determination. Nothing was ever undercooked.

My letters resumed in October 2010 when my mother fell for a second time, this time breaking her right arm. As I resumed the email messages, they evolved into an ante-mortem eulogy. I was reminded of Garrison Keillor's story of a funeral where the eulogy was so wonderful that everyone expressed sadness that the deceased was unable to hear it. And he only missed it by a few days! I set my sights on achieving that.

I turned the initial email letters into blog posts, allowing me to include photographs and other descriptive material. Compared to the usual, modern means of communicating with family and friends using social media, I found this approach more contemplative and slow moving. I hope the stories about my mother and my family will be generalizable to others outside the immediate family as I offer this book as a way to celebrate the remarkable life of my mother. The many contributions of my father and my three siblings to the story make clear the magnitude of the challenges faced by families in dealing with a person who has Alzheimer's disease. The journey is not only arduous, but it is long: These letters began when Maggie first fell in December 2009 and conclude after her death on January 21, 2015, more than five years later.

As I looked back on these 87 posts, I realized I would have liked to have been able to find such support in a book when my family and I were learning how to care for first one, and then a second, parent with cognitive decline. I found myself adding more material to the blogs, material that might explain our story to non-family members and adding more of what is known about Alzheimer's disease. Turning the email letters into blog postings and then into book content gave me a vehicle to express the life lessons I have learned from my mother and the rest of my family. In them, I write as a son, a physician and an aspiring scientist. As the spiritual journey was such an important part of my upbringing, I also weave in my own perspective and the insights gained from a 23-year participation in a group for meditation, study and contemplative discussion.

Finally, let me offer the suggestion to incorporate writing in your life if you haven't already. I have found comfort in writing throughout time. I suggest that you write about your situation and your emotions. If you have a family member with an illness or Alzheimer's disease, you might use writing as a way to discover and focus on what the patient can still do. Meyer Freidman, M.D., the originator of the idea of the Type A personality 40 years ago, proposed letter writing as an antidote to the intensity of the Type A personality.[2] From my perspective, I noticed the difference between my usual way of observing an event and witnessing the same thing with enough attention to write to my family about it afterward. Letter writing can introduce a contemplative element into any part of the day. At one point, I made a pledge to write at least two letters a month, so I often found myself starting the day with "beginner's mind," as I sought a fresh perspective on the morning and the events that followed. If you choose not to share your thoughts with others through letters, it is just as therapeutic to set time aside to put your recollections of and thoughts about events into a journal.

Both of my parents were fond of the poetry of Henry van Dyke (1852-1933). In the quiet that gave rise to this memoir, I yearned for a kindness of heart that is summarized in this line of van Dyke's from "The Foot-Path to Peace:"[3]

> *"Be glad of life because it gives you the chance to love*
> *and to work and to play and to look up at the stars."*

— Felix

CHAPTER ONE

Maggie's Fall Starts It All

DECEMBER 12, 2009, 8:56 A.M.

Dear Family,

Maggie fell on the way into the medical office building yesterday morning. I got there just in time to see the chaos develop. She had tripped on a bit of slightly raised concrete and landed facedown. It was about 20 degrees with a strong north wind, so everybody was cold, and it must have been very cold lying on the sidewalk. She was soon covered with so many blankets nobody could see how serious her injuries were. Even though this happened just outside our cardiac catheterization laboratory, and the lab personnel arrived immediately with a stretcher, someone at the hospital determined that the rescue team needed to be called. Trenton Fire took her to the emergency room on the other side of the building.

In the ER, she got a lot of things she didn't need, and also got very good and concerned care from some clearly professional personnel. The head CAT scan (CT) showed no bleeding or skull fracture, and the neck CT showed no break, so she was taken out of the cervical collar. She does have a fracture of the left elbow. There is a break just a little bit away from the end of the ulnar bone. She has so much osteoporosis that her triceps muscle pulled the bone fragment of the tip away from the rest of the bone. The good news is that she doesn't have two raw edges of bone rubbing against each other, so she doesn't have much pain. The bad news is that it will take an open surgical procedure to reattach the bone. This is scheduled for Monday.

Dad took her home from the hospital about 5 p.m. yesterday, with the arm in a sling. I would guess that she will need to be in a cast or a sling for six to eight weeks after the surgery. I'll update you about that when I know.

I haven't called yet this morning for an update, but I'll let you all know what I know as I can.

— Felix

DECEMBER 12, 2009, 10:08 A.M.

Dear Family,

Here's an update since my note earlier this morning. Maggie fell out of bed at 9 p.m. last night. Dad was unable to get her back in bed, so he had to call the fire department. They got her into a chair on rollers and then into the twin bed in the guest bedroom.

This morning Dad got up and didn't see her in bed. She had fallen to the floor again, and he was again unable to get her back into bed. He's just not strong enough. He called Brian, the handyman, who came straight over.

I'm heading down to try to help. It seems to me that the best option may be a nursing home for a few weeks or a live-in helper. I'll get some advice from Valerie, who's been there, done that. Not only is Dad too weak to help pick Maggie up, he probably can't hear her when she calls.

I'll try to be in email contact. If you call my cell at the folks' after 11 a.m., I'll be there most of the day.

— Felix

DECEMBER 12, 2009, 3:30 P.M.

Dear Family,

It's 3:30 p.m. here on Parke Lane at the folks' house. I got here four hours ago. Maggie was on the commode and couldn't get up. Dad couldn't help her. It took me so much effort that the theory I composed in the car ride down here seems to be confirmed: Maggie must have suffered a stroke in the last week or two. Dad said that she has been falling a lot during that time period. The CT scan yesterday showed evidence of a stroke in the basal ganglia and the putamen. These are the same areas of the brain affected by Parkinson's disease, and they affect the ability to walk. Yesterday, I just assumed that these were chronic findings on the CT scan. Now it makes more sense that she fell yesterday because of this new stroke.

I am grateful to Valerie Overholt (our next-door neighbor from childhood and also a physician), who has been through this with her mother. Together, Val and I have developed a game plan. I'll spend the night tonight. Tomorrow, Ann, who did such a great job taking care of Val's mother Vivian, will spend the night. Monday, Maggie will have surgery on her left elbow. We'll then plan an admission to the hospital and get proper neurology and physical therapy evaluations. I would hope that she would then be transferred to a rehab unit for a couple of weeks. Dad has agreed to employ home care after that.

It's hauntingly quiet here on Parke Lane. The folks do not listen to the radio or turn on the TV. Brian fixed the leaking faucet in the kitchen after he got Maggie up off the floor this morning. We ate lunch while he finished his work. Maggie drifts off to sleep a lot, then opens her eyes, looks about and drifts off again. Since it's one of the shortest days of the year, the sun is low in the sky, and there are no clouds. The Detroit River to the east is ruffled by a steady wind from the south, and it's warmed up to about 25 degrees. The dead tree at Jeanette McCauley's house next door has been blown down in the last day or two, and the dead branches and rotten roots block part of our view of the river. Dad sits quietly and doesn't read. In many ways, it's so serene that I don't feel like reading either.

But, I am a Rogers, so I'm going to go scrub their toilets now. Few things promise to be so invigorating.

— Felix

DECEMBER 13, 2009, 11:18 A.M.

Dear Family,

Things are a little better this morning. Dad and I cooked dinner last night: roasted chicken, parsnips and succotash. It was plausible, if not delectable. I've converted the chicken carcass into chicken soup for lunch today, and Dad had me cook a real farm breakfast this morning: bacon, eggs, toast and applesauce. To save me typing time, I'll just add now that every food item started with the word "organic."

I slept in the guest room with twin beds so I could keep an eye on Maggie. In spite of that, she was gone when I awoke at 7 a.m. She had made her way back to the master bedroom. Dad was asleep on the couch, so he could be closer, but also because the environmentally safe product used to clean the porch off the master bedroom causes him an allergic reaction.

So while it's good that she can sometimes get up on her own, it makes for unpredictability. We had to offer four or five times to help her get up from the breakfast table before she finally got it. I think that experience was helpful in convincing Dad that he can't take care of Maggie, even during daylight hours. The episode convinced me of the strong human desire to have purpose in our lives. After each time that Maggie tried but failed to get up out of her chair, she carefully rearranged the napkins and the mail on the breakfast table as if she had really intended to do that instead.

I am trying to handle a few of the delicate topics. Dad does think that he has legal power of attorney, and he's going to look for those documents today. Ann is coming here between 1-2 p.m. She charges $8-$10 an hour daytime, $15 an hour at night. That's about $300/day, $9,000 a month. Dad didn't think it would be a problem, since "this won't be for a long time."

This house could be a demonstration project for fall risk: poor lighting, throw rugs everywhere, small tables that would not support you if you leaned on them, clutter everywhere. The cleaning lady can't see and doesn't wear her glasses. After my triumph in the toilets yesterday, I was set to do the vacuuming. Turns out they don't have a vacuum cleaner at the moment; the cleaning lady's husband is going to fix it "mañana." Where will I find my sense of purpose?

I'll write again after Ann gets here. It ain't over until the homecare person signs on.

— Felix

DECEMBER 13, 2009, 7 P.M.

Dear Family,

Here's an update: I met Ann at 2 p.m. today. She is remarkably sweet, with obvious patience and a real sense of serenity. We talked a bit about what she does, and her fee schedule. It turns out I was wrong. It's even more expensive. The daytime fee is $18 an hour; the night is $15 an hour. Dad still went for it. Ann started today, and she'll stay until Dad takes Maggie to the hospital about noon tomorrow.

Then we all talked about the anticipated schedule. Unlike the agreement I thought we had reached yesterday, Dad wants to take Maggie home from the hospital immediately after surgery. He did agree to the idea of a consult with a neurologist and with a physical medicine specialist and then rehab. But only after Maggie seems ready for it and only as outpatient. This is completely unrealistic. Dad and I first went toe-to-toe, then chin-to-chin, and ran out of anatomy before we had a meeting of the minds. Ann sat by calmly, and Maggie wasn't sure what was happening, but she must have wondered why we were talking so loud.

Not until hours later did I remember the insight a nurse taught me years ago. When a patient (or a patient's family) is disagreeable or irrational, it's usually because they are afraid. Perhaps if I'd had more awareness of this during my talk with Dad, I would have been less confrontational. Of course, Dad's fear is a complex issue. He's genuinely fearful on Maggie's behalf, and he's also afraid of losing control, of having an empty house, and there may be many more issues that we will never know about since he is so secretive about things like this.

I have kept the office up to date on all this. It's been disruptive for them as well. All of those who knew of my mother's fall were of great comfort to me, and their words, or even glances of concern, were much appreciated. In particular, Brenda and Gail were of tremendous help on the scene, for which my father and I are very thankful.

I will be calling the surgeon prior to Maggie's surgery to make arrangements for him to admit Maggie to the hospital and to arrange the necessary consultations. I think it would be helpful if everyone reinforced the value of this strategy. Maggie really needs inpatient treatment after surgery for reasons that include the fact that it will allow her to qualify for home nursing and physical therapy care. It was helpful that Howard and Val came by just as Dad and I were wrapping up this discussion. They and Ann commented on how much Vivian benefited from the rehab experience. They acknowledged that she was more confused for a while in the unfamiliar setting of the rehab unit, but that the benefits of the experience far outweighed the temporary confusion.

I have the feeling that Dad may have already reneged on our plan of care that we agreed upon yesterday. That makes me concerned that he may also drop Ann prematurely. I think we just need to be as supportive as we can be.

— Felix

DECEMBER 14, 2009, 9:40 P.M.

Dear Family,

Maggie had successful surgery today. Jody stayed with Dad during the surgery, and then I spent some time with Maggie after Dad left. She's very stable medically and in good spirits. She didn't know why she was in the hospital or how long she had been there, but she was comfortable in her setting.

Ann called me today with two items of concern. First, that Dad had called her and told her that he would be bringing Maggie home at noon tomorrow. Second, that Dad had a falling episode last night. Ann was right there, of course, and helped with the abrasion he had suffered on his elbow. He told her it was likely that it was a reaction to her perfume. Ann doesn't wear perfume.

Ann said she could be available tomorrow at noon, but that she could not arrange 24-hour coverage until at least 10 days from now. In addition, she recommended that the house be prepared for a disabled person: toilet risers, support bars in the bathrooms, etc. In addition, they need proper lighting in the house: Nearly all of the lights are the type where you need to lean in to turn the switch under the lampshade. Not the best type for a person with precarious balance. We might as well place whoopee cushions on the floor underneath them, so at least Jody and I will have something to laugh about when the person falls.

I've presented this to Dad as a non-negotiable situation. The house is not safe for Maggie at present, no one is available to provide her care for at least 10 days, and Dad really needs to get some rest before he has a more serious falling spell. I called Ann and told her that we will not need her tomorrow. Now there is no turning back. I talked quite a bit about rehab with Maggie tonight. I don't think she would mind it, especially if we point out that we really don't have any other option (except a nursing home). Dad told Lisa that they would be taking Maggie to rehab "as long as that's what she wants."

So, on to rehab chic. Val went through all the clothes that Sheila and Dad had sorted out to donate to the Salvation Army. She rescued several items of retro-fashion that might have some use and a very nice jacket that Maggie has probably forgotten about. Val also alerted my wife, Caroline, to Appleseed catalogue. It's filled with clothing ideas for older people, modeled by impossibly attractive and wholesome appearing women in their early 30s. Working with a budget of $400, Caroline has found a series of items that Val says are the preferred attire for rehab and home afterward, items that look like jogging suits, but with button-up blouses and pull-up slacks with elastic or drawstring waistbands. The exact opposite of what she is wearing at the moment. The catalog items are appropriate for a person with an elbow injury, for example.

If the four Rogers kids want to go in on this, the new clothes can be our Christmas gift to Maggie, and we can get the order shipped here in time for her to start in rehab.

— Felix

DECEMBER 16, 2009

Dear Family,

Things seem to be going well here at the hospital. After Maggie had surgery Monday, she slept through the night. Tuesday she was animated throughout the day. I think she may have gotten over-stimulated because she got so restless at night that they had to call in a sitter to keep an eye on her. She received a minor sedative and, consequently, didn't wake up in time for breakfast. Today, she was also animated. In fact, you'll never guess what occupied much of her attention: watching TV!

The neurology and physical therapy evaluations have been completed, but I haven't had the chance to look them over, except to know that Maggie is not a candidate for the rehab program at Wyandotte. She's too healthy in terms of her elbow injury. As of this afternoon, the staff was applying to Belle Fountain, a new sub-acute rehabilitation facility in Riverview that is getting strongly positive reviews from patients and their families. She just got transferred from the Observation Unit to Room 412, where she will probably be until she leaves for Belle Fountain. The ward secretary just called me with that news, adding that Maggie was talking to everybody on the unit about going to Arizona. She's charmed them all, despite the fact that her conversation is largely incoherent.

I think it's great to see Maggie around so many other people and even to see her enjoy television. I think she may have had a component of sensory deprivation at home on Parke Lane. Apart from her social interaction at the office, she does not have many visitors, watches no television and does not even listen to much music. I think the idea of exercising our brains is good, but it seems that she may have passed the point of recovery and renewal.

Enjoyment of entertainment and happiness from the association with other people may be much more appropriate goals at this stage. Of course, Dad has really tried in this regard. But, they have outlived most of their friends. And, Maggie was the social force years ago, not Dad.

I'll write again when any other developments occur.

— Felix

DECEMBER 17, 2009

Dear Family,

Over the last several days with Maggie, I have been reminded of the writer Dylan Thomas, in ways that reflect on my introduction to him in college. About this time of the year, for each of my last three years at school, my roommates and I would listen to Richard Burton on an old LP (long-play, 33-1/3 rpm) vinyl record, reading "A Child's Christmas in Wales,"[4] but only after Don Stokes had arranged the lighting, called for quiet and otherwise made sure that each of us were imbued with his own sense that something special was about to happen.

Over the weekend, I reminded Maggie of my favorite part in that long story. There was a fire at a house one Christmas. Miss Prothero had a reputation that she always knew the right thing to say. After young Dylan and his friend Jim helped to extinguish the fire by throwing snowballs in the living room, and the firemen had come out on Christmas day to put the fire out, here's how Dylan Thomas described the right thing:

> *"Jim's aunt, Miss Prothero, came downstairs and peered in at them. Jim and I waited, very quietly, to hear what she would say to them. She said the right thing, always. She looked at the three tall firemen in their shining helmets, standing among the smoke and cinders and dissolving snowballs, and she said, 'Would you like anything to read?'"*

When I recounted this story, Maggie didn't remember the year when, around Thanksgiving, we had to call the fire department because our living room filled with smoke. I always did feel that Maggie would be likely to offer everyone a cup of tea in a similar circumstance. We could also always turn to her for the right thing to say. Now her speech mostly expresses a rambling concern for where she is, what will happen next, when she will get back to Grosse Ile, and isolated references to Tucson and Vancouver. She is concerned that there are people we need to thank and others we owe something to before she can leave for home. Even so, she has moved to a new floor in the hospital, and the staff here is equally charmed by her. Everyone is impressed by her sweetness.

My second concern with Dylan Thomas recalls my first year in college. We had a very gifted tenor in the senior class, and a surprising surplus of trombonists, me included. The decision was made to present a special concert with a work for tenor and four trombones, making use of the text of "Do Not Go Gentle into That Good Night," by Dylan Thomas.[5] Of course, as a freshman at the start of protests against the war in Vietnam, I was all about "Rage, rage against the dying of the light."

Now, as I look at Maggie in the twilight of her life, I don't feel that she is living out that sentiment or that it would be in any way appropriate. Despite her inability to pull together thoughts or memories, her serenity is the most impressive thing about her as she sits in the chair, often for long periods without speaking. Her demeanor, facial expressions and upright posture still convey her sense of dignity. She seems intent on expressing her concern.

Having rejected the rage idea, instead I see Maggie coming close to embracing the night, as Dylan Thomas describes at the end of "A Child's Christmas in Wales":

> "… and then I went to bed. Looking through my bedroom window, out into the moonlight and the unending smoke-colored snow, I could see the lights in the windows of all the other houses on our hill and hear the music rising from them up the long, steady falling night. I turned the gas down, I got into bed. I said some words to the close and holy darkness, and then I slept."

— Felix

DECEMBER 18, 2009

Dear Family,

Maggie was transferred to Belle Fountain this afternoon. I got there about 6:45, just as she was getting back to her room. Dad was there at the time. She had a short intake assessment by the physical therapist, and then Dad left.

She protested as Dad left, and then she kept on with her protest while I was there. It was good to see her pulling more thoughts together, even if they were opposed to our treatment plan. The director of physical therapy, Greg Guyon, M.D., came in when I was there. He has a nice way with people. He was friendly and not challenging to Maggie. When I left, I met Ralph Raper, M.D., the medical director. I've known him for years. I gave him a short rundown on Maggie's history. He's looking forward to being very supportive.

Maggie continued to complain that she wanted to go home to Grosse Ile. I took her for a few walks up and down the long hall. She got to talk to Jody on the phone and that helped calm her down. About 8:15, she abruptly said, "You need to let me go down the hall a few rooms, so I can go to bed." I told her we were in her bedroom, and she became very relieved. I helped brush her teeth and "go winkie," and then I tucked her into bed. She was asleep 15 minutes later.

I think I ended up as the night watchman because Dad just doesn't feel comfortable with the role of explaining to Maggie that she must be in the rehab center. The center is very nice, and I can see that physical therapy is a major focus for them. The staff is friendly and seems competent.

She's hoping to see Lisa and her dog Bentley tomorrow.

— Felix

CHAPTER TWO

Intermezzo. A Pause When Things Seem to be Normal

LISA AND BENTLEY ARRIVED FROM CLEVELAND late the following afternoon. Bentley is a Bedlington terrier from a championship show line. In Lisa's eyes, he is not just well behaved—he's aristocratic. We usually just caved and agreed to call him "Lord" Bentley. On the other hand, Maggie just welcomes him with a cheerful smile and a firm ruffle to his head of curly hair. Except for the brief reign of Mr. Lim, our Siamese cat, Maggie was a dog person through and through.

Our first dog was Tammy, a Scottish terrier. My brother claims that Scotties were the choice of the previous owners of the house. Lisa tells me that Tammy was a gift to Maggie from the well-intentioned, but clueless, wife of the local cardiac surgeon. She wanted to give Maggie a gift to celebrate Lisa's birth, her fourth child in six years, and a puppy seemed like "just the right thing." Things were so hectic that Tammy slept in a dresser drawer until my parents had the time to get a proper bed for the puppy. I assumed that the Scottish terrier was chosen to lead off the menagerie because of my mother's heritage.

Maggie's father ran a laundry in Paisley, Scotland. His father-in-law

Here Pierre, our Great Pyrenees who replaced Tammy, looks on skeptically as Jody holds Giselle, the new puppy and also a Great Pyrenees.

had been a prominent real estate developer and had tenement homes as rental properties. The laundry never really supported the family, and all of his father-in-law's properties were new and not generating income. The family elected to immigrate to Canada. His brother-in-law, Cameron Barr, had a fruit ranch in Summerland, in the Okanagan Valley of British Columbia. They settled with him and later bought a 20-acre fruit farm of their own.

Work on the farm was hard with no frills. The family made toys out of discarded wood. One of the most exciting events for them was to ride in the snow on a horse-drawn sled. They kept warm with heavy blankets and the heat from large, smooth rocks, which they had warmed at the hearth and placed at their feet. In her early childhood, Maggie studied piano and was apparently talented. Although

Maggie's father, Alexander McGown, in Vancouver.

she would rarely comment on it, Dad told us she won a national piano competition when she was 4 or 5 years old.

Then came the Great Depression. Young men rode the rails to get to the Canadian cities in hopes of finding work, not knowing there were unemployed professionals waiting ahead of them in the lines at the soup kitchens. Maggie's family moved about 250 miles west to Vancouver, where her father went to work in the laundry of the Empress Hotel.

When Maggie was about 18, she followed her two older brothers, Cameron and Alastair, to medical school. In those days, undergraduate college was not a prerequisite. They were inspired to attend the Kirksville College of Osteopathy and Surgery because their "Auntie Mabel" (who must have been a relative of my maternal grandmother) had graduated from the Kirksville school before returning to Ayr, Scotland. And, just in time, Maggie's maternal grandfather sent the first installment of rental income from Scotland to pay their tuition, which was $90 a semester. Maggie worked in the laundry and was paid 29 cents an hour. She recalled making $29 the summer before she left for medical school; it met her incidental expenses for the entire year.

My father grew up in a small coal-mining town in West Virginia where his father ran the appliance store. My dad's two older sisters were highly competent women with advanced degrees in education and psychology. He was inspired to attend the Kirksville school after meeting several charismatic, peripatetic educators who passed through town. Dad played trumpet in a local jazz band to make ends meet. My parents met in medical school.

Each of my parents was highly accomplished. In the early 1940s, my mother was the first woman to complete an internship in the osteopathic profession and went on to a distinguished career in family practice and internal medicine.

My father was a well-regarded specialist in cardiology who turned his practice interests to environmental medicine in his later years. I took him aside in 2005 when I learned that he and my mother had been named Great Pioneers in Osteopathic Medicine, and the reporters would be interviewing each of them for the profession's national magazine and website. I was so worried that my mother's cognitive decline would not only become public, but also be a source of embarrassment to all involved. Dad reassured me that Mom could practice her answers, and the reporters would edit them favorably before publication. He was right.

My parents moved to Alexandria, Virginia, after they completed

Left: Joseph T. Rogers, aka JTR, Joe, "Dad" about 1945;   Right: Maggie in 1950

their training in medicine because my father had been recruited to help establish a hospital. That proved to be too formidable, so they moved to the Detroit area in 1948, and then settled on Grosse Ile in 1950. They chose a large home on the west side of the island with 300 feet of waterfront on the Detroit River.

A few years later, Maggie's parents moved in with us. Apparently, her father, Alexander, could no longer maintain the laundry and may have had a drinking problem. My brother recalls that he had heart failure, possibly due to valvular aortic stenosis, for which there was no surgical treatment at the time. He became seriously short of breath after climbing just one flight of steps. He died soon after he moved in with us.

Maggie's mother, Jane, at that time was experiencing significant

Left: Maggie and Joseph Rogers, Jane and Alexander McGown;
Right: Maggie's mother, Jane McGown, about 1938

cognitive decline. While I don't remember Maggie's father at all, I do recall one incident with my maternal grandmother. By this time, both of my younger sisters had been born. One summer day, my grandmother disappeared. She was found a couple of miles from our house. She had tucked a baby doll into the perambulator (or "baby buggy," as we called it), and wandered off down the street. There were no sidewalks, so she was literally walking in the street. She was found in such a state of bewilderment that this event became a family emergency. Maggie had four young children (and a dog), and I doubt it would have been feasible to think she could care for all of us and her mother, so her mother was placed in a small residence home in Windsor, Ontario, where my parents were able to visit her periodically.

I have a vivid memory of us four children being called to Maggie's bedroom one morning. The room was unlit. From her seat on the bench at her vanity table, she turned and addressed us. In a calm voice, she matter-of-factly told us that her mother had just died. I remember feeling numb and unsure of how I should react. I was 10 years old and had barely known this grandmother. I also hadn't known anyone who had died before, and I had no context to understand what it meant, especially to my mother. I remember that we children did not cry, probably did not offer words of consolation, and quietly left the room. I do not remember attending the funeral, but my sister Sheila has told me that we did, as she remembers Maggie in tears at the graveside.

Our childhood was otherwise completely idyllic. We had a beautiful home on a large property with gardens and outbuildings including a stable, a chicken coop and a greenhouse. A couple lived in the apartment over the garage. The wife did housekeeping, and the husband helped with the yard work and maintenance. Our two next-door neighbors had children our age who were perfect playmates. We were a self-contained neighborhood and lacked nothing.

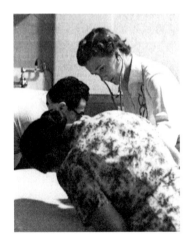

Left: "Doctor Sheila," as she was known - 1950s; Right: Sunset Lodge, our home on Grosse Ile, soon after it was built, about 1925

Growing up, I had no idea that my mother was a pioneer in any way because she was just our mom. Years later, when feminism was widespread and women became much more accepted in medicine, she tended to brush off her accomplishments, as if it would be making too much of the obvious. For quite a few years, she gave up the practice of medicine to be a stay-at-home mom. While I was in high school, she provided emergency coverage for a family physician who had developed a sudden health problem, and then she maintained that practice for years after his death. After she left that practice, she took on the position as volunteer physician for the Salvation Army in downtown Detroit, working primarily in the alcoholic treatment program. Despite not understanding the "tough" part of tough love, she was named their volunteer of the year in 1973.

Maggie also enjoyed small, focused projects that she could do when moved by the spirit. I planted a peace pole at Christ Church Cranbrook in 1985. She liked the idea and arranged for the dedication of a peace pole at St. James Church on Grosse Isle. Soon after, she had given peace poles to groups throughout the Detroit area. After she met Samir Kafity, the Anglican Bishop of Jerusalem, she arranged for a peace pole to be sent to Jerusalem, and she was thrilled to get his letter of thanks. She ended up with widespread distribution of these gifts, including a pole on the Trans-Canada highway in northern Ontario and in Cape Town, South Africa, after her meeting with Bishop Desmond Tutu.

Maggie typically made her own dresses for fancy occasions. She often saved a bit of the material to make a bow tie for Dad.

At home, Maggie supervised four children whose ages spanned just six years. My parents held high expectations for each of us, in music, sports, including cheerleading for the girls, and, of course, academic achievement. Maggie taught my sisters how to sew, and they made their own dresses on occasion.

When we were older, we came to appreciate her cooking. As children of the Great Depression, my parents were cautious about living in any way that resembled a pampered lifestyle; it was distinctly rare for us to go out to a restaurant. On the other hand, Maggie did indulge herself with a subscription to *Gourmet* magazine. My wife recalls Maggie's decision to cook an engagement party dinner for the two of us. Caroline watched the cookbooks fly off the shelves. Then Maggie and Lisa began picking out recipes, making shopping lists, and later, embarking on the meal preparation. When it was all laid out, we enjoyed a sumptuous strolling dinner with food from diverse countries served buffet-style. There may have been 20 or 30 people invited to the party, and not once was there any talk of getting a caterer or relying on any other support.

Maggie's greatest source of satisfaction was her life in the church. She was raised Presbyterian and my father was a Methodist. They agreed on the Episcopal Church as a compromise. Our local church was St. James, which began with a picturesque chapel founded by a runaway slave who escaped across the Detroit River to Canada, living there for five years to procure her freedom.

My parents were fully involved in church life. They taught Sunday school, sang in the choir, served on church committees, and Maggie was a staunch member of the Episcopal Church Women, serving as its president. She liked to do things "just right." When she was president, she started each meeting by reading from Robert's Rules of Order. She was surprised to learn that other presidents had not followed this pattern. My father was on the vestry, the church leadership organization, and he was the chair of the Memorial Garden Committee. My parents' contribution to the garden was a tri-colored beech tree, whose roots now support the ashes of them both.

CHAPTER THREE

Maggie Falls Again

OCTOBER 17, 2010

Dear Family,

Maggie has fallen again.

Today has been one of those beautiful October days here in Michigan: crisp air, clear blue sky with fair-weather cumulus clouds drifting across, temperatures a few degrees above normal. Dad and Maggie went out about 2 p.m. to pick vegetables for dinner. Usually this is well-coordinated, but today Maggie ventured ahead without waiting for assistance to get down the short step from the patio. She fell, injuring her right shoulder.

Dad was unable to get her up. To avoid calling 911, he called me. Fortunately, I was just 10 minutes away, having just left work for their house.

We went to the emergency room, where our stay was brief and efficient. Maggie sustained a fracture to the upper portion of her right humerus, close to the shoulder joint. It will not need surgery, so we were discharged two hours ago. She should be safely home by now. I asked Jody to keep an eye out for the car, so he can help them into the house.

Throughout all of this, Maggie was a trouper. I know the modern word for this is "warrior," but trouper is more like the word Maggie would have used. She didn't ask for any pain medicine. Several times she asked where she was or how far we were from the hospital where I work. I think, to her, her disorientation was as troubling as the fracture. Her arm should be in a sling for a few weeks. We'll know more after she sees the orthopedic surgeon Tuesday.

Years ago, Maggie used to chide Dad about his obsessive-compulsive behavior, which we wisely attributed to the fact that he was born under the sign of Virgo. She said a Virgo will stop to put a pin back in its place before fleeing a burning house. I had occasion to remember that today. I helped Maggie up after her fall and walked her to the car, trying to straighten her dress and arrange her disheveled hair. Dad held the car door for us. As we walked, he had time to carefully pull the leaves out from the front part of the windshield behind the edge of the hood. The car was ready when we got there.

I want you to know the family dynamics were most calm today. It was quiet in the emergency room, and neither my father nor I had anything in particular on our schedules, so we experienced a placid waiting period for the X-rays and other aspects of medical care.

Both Maggie and Dad are sure they can cope with this annoyance without as much as a ruffle in the fabric of their day. This is remarkable, considering that it means a 90-year-old man, who still intends to get to work on time tomorrow, is caring for a 92-year-old woman with advanced dementia.

But, cope they do. Consider this. The accident happened in the afternoon, and the good news is that it allowed Maggie to give Dad a haircut this morning, before her right arm was put out of commission. It is a surprisingly good haircut, and he no longer looks like the second-place runner-up in the Howard Hughes look-alike contest. I say surprising because at teatime yesterday, Maggie stared at the bowl of strawberries 6 inches in front of her asking, "What are these?" Her macular degeneration has progressed seriously, which likely played a part in her fall.

I have added a new name to my email distribution list of family, Jamie Jackson, our cousin from Melbourne, Australia. Jamie, I welcome you to these letters. I hope that you don't find this too obscure, since you missed the first series of The Maggie Letters, when she broke her left elbow last December. We all still hope that we can set the date for your visit here after the first of the year, and you may as well have some of this background before your arrival. Please forward this to your sister Sally if you think she would be interested.

I'll try to keep all of you informed.

— Felix

NOVEMBER 9, 2010

Dear Family,

   This note harkens to the newspaper adage that good news isn't news at all; after all, we don't hear about the airplane that lands safely each day. Now three weeks after my letter to you all about Maggie's latest injury, I do think I need to add a few words of good news.

   I have been by to see Maggie a few times since she fell on October 17th, and Sheila has been up from Oklahoma to spend some time. I was at the house on Parke Lane this past weekend. Maggie isn't wearing a sling, and while she has a limited range of motion with her right arm, her pain seems to be controlled. She does well eating with her left hand. She should start to make faster progress when she starts physical therapy this week.

   Just as I got there this past Saturday, a huge, bright blue freighter from Beluga Products was making its way past their house. They do have a fabulous view. Seagulls careened against a murky, gray-blue fall sky, and a band of robins moved in and out of the birdbath on their patio. They were at teatime when I arrived. Maggie was pert and attentive. It did take a while for her to fully realize who I was.

   She was wearing an ancient kilt with a large, uncomplicated pin on the left side and a cambric blouse with a large collar. Sheila tells me that Dad had started getting these old kilts out when she was visiting. They do make a nice statement. It's fun to remember those times. Lisa and Sheila used to spend time going over the choice of large safety pins used to hold their kilts together. I remember decorative ones, and the cachet they added to the outfits.

   We moved straight from teatime to dinner. Dad has a formula for mealtime, and it works. He starts the beans from his garden as if he were still in the South, giving them enough time to cook, and then four more hours just for good measure. He's stopped using the regular oven and just uses the toaster oven to cook the yams. He cooks the salmon on call for the meal, and it turns out to be tender.[6] Dessert is also cooked in the toaster oven, apples roasted with a bit of cinnamon.

   Once at the table, Dad asked me to say grace, but Maggie didn't hear him ask, so she went ahead. Here's what she said: "Lord, we have so much to be thankful for. And, unless we tell you, we won't believe it to be true."

I remember asking once about a person we visited during my childhood, Auntie Clark, a Boston dowager whose manner was larger

than life. Dad explained that as we get older, "whatever we are, we become more so." I'm pleased to report how this is true for my parents. Their abiding love and tenderness for one another is touching, and permanent. They are very much alone with one another now, having outlived just about all their friends. Their house is quiet and calm. They have a routine that suits them just fine. They make accommodations for one another's needs and cares that seem just right: Dad is doting and

Auntie Clark at Rondeau

concerned; Maggie is equally attentive to what she can do.

All seems well at the moment. I'll be in touch.

— Felix

NOVEMBER 10, 2010

Dear Family,

Last July, around the time of Maggie's birthday, I stopped at the house for a visit. She was in the chair where she always sits, by the front door. It was unusual that she didn't get up when I came in. I sat down on the rattan chair across from her and asked what she was reading. She answered, "I don't know, but whatever it is, it doesn't make any sense." She handed me the book. It was "The Book of Common Prayer," open to the calendar of saints. There in the smallest font imaginable was a list of the saints for each of the dates designated by the Anglican Church. There are lots of blank dates, and those that are listed include some odd names, like Remigius, and Ephrem of Edessa. Not that any of that really mattered, given the font size and her vision problems.

Later that day I was shopping for a new phone. Across the street was a religious bookstore. Since Maggie is so hard to shop for, I figured that I had the perfect birthday gift. I bought a giant (not large, but giant) print edition of the Bible and gave it to her a day or two later.

When I stopped by yesterday, I looked at the neat row of books by her chair. Right in front was "The Book of Common Prayer." Tucked a little further away was the Bible I had given her. At least it had a bookmark in it, so she might be reading it on occasion.

Maggie's prayer life has always been an important part of her daily routine. As kids, we started each day by practicing our musical instruments while she made breakfast. Then at breakfast we read from the illustrated "Hurlbut's Story of the Bible" or some other text. When we were in Canada together a couple years ago, I was very moved by the intensity of Maggie's evening prayers. I wonder how her devotions have evolved with her progressive cognitive decline.

It brings to mind a short story of Leo Tolstoy's, "The Three Hermits." A bishop of the Orthodox Church is sailing with a group of pilgrims to the Solovetsky Monastery. En route, they have the chance to stop at an isolated island where there are three hermit monks. The bishop decides to visit the island and assist the men in their prayer lives.

The monks are very old and have long beards; they are bent over or toothless, or both. The bishop discovers that the three monks claim they do not know how to serve God. Instead, each day they pray, "Three are ye, three are we, have mercy on us." The bishop recognizes that they have heard of the Holy Trinity, but they "do not pray aright."

Painstakingly, he teaches them the Lord's Prayer. He spends all day long teaching them this prayer.

As the ship left the island, they could hear the men repeating the Lord's Prayer. When the island was long out of sight, something shining was seen on the waves. As it drew closer, it was recognized to be the three hermits, gliding across the water.

> *"All three as with one voice, began to say: 'We have forgotten your teaching … Teach us again.'*
> *The Bishop crossed himself, and leaning over the ship's side, said: 'Your own prayer will reach the Lord, men of God. It is not for me to teach you. Pray for us sinners.'*
> *And the Bishop bowed low before the old men; and they turned and went back across the sea. And a light shone until daybreak on the spot where they were lost to sight."[7]*

So much effort can be devoted to the contemplative life. And it is a discipline. But for Maggie, it's such an ingrained part of her that such a contemplative life seems to be immune to the ravages of dementia. I find myself hoping that this is what I will achieve. I can hope that, no matter what happens, the connection with the Spirit will be the one permanent aspect of who I am.

 — Felix

NOVEMBER 20, 2010

Dear Family,

 I saw Maggie at work yesterday. As often happens, it was in the middle of a busy morning with patients. I saw her at the front desk, which was crowded with other patients checking in and out. We only talked for a few minutes. She had just come from her vitamin infusion, which Dad arranges for her as an alternative to Aricept and those other medicines that don't work but are widely employed for the treatment of Alzheimer's dementia. (This statement reflects my father's opinion of Aricept (donepezil), which I dutifully reported at the time. Please see the *Notes* for the report of the *Lancet* Commission on Dementia.[8]) Maggie and Dad stood with Stephanie, her caregiver, and Gail, the infusion nurse. Stephanie is tall and wholesome, with a fresh smile and a caring manner. Gail has the confident persona of a really good nurse. We came to appreciate both of them greatly.

 Caroline had found some cookies for Maggie and sent them down with me. Caroline was pleased to have found some gluten-free cookies that seemed to meet all of the food dyscrasias in the Rogers house. I had delivered them earlier in the week, and the folks called Thursday to express thanks, but I was at a meeting and missed the call. Here's how our conversation this day went:

 "Maggie, Caroline said you called about the cookies she sent down."

 "I did?"

 "Yes, she said that you really enjoyed the cookies."

 "I did? Well, that's good."

 Her smile was pleasing. Her face was attentive. Her skin is so deeply furrowed that the lipstick makes its way into the tiny interstices around her mouth and blurs its margins.

 One of the fruits of friendship is that we remember gifts of kindness and generosity, and we respond with thanks. It's hard to resist the expression of thanks as a litmus test of a relationship.

Earlier this week, Caroline and I counted up some of the friends who had been to our house multiple times and never once invited us to their house. This was in response to needing to decide if we were going to throw a holiday party, as well as to test our own commitment to the Christmas spirit.

Of course, remembering kind actions and expressing thanks or reciprocating acts of love changes as the relationship matures. During the courtship phase of a romantic relationship, I suspect that the professions of love may outweigh the strength of the love, and years later the relationship may be rock solid with few words or gifts exchanged.

For Maggie, of course, remembering is no longer part of the equation.

This week, our weekly church study group addresses the challenging story of Jesus and the fig tree.[9] Jesus is hungry, but as the tree is out of the season of bearing fruit, no figs are to be found on the tree. He curses the tree for not bearing fruit, and it withers. This is quite a shocking story, especially for those of us who see Jesus as always loving.

Mary Gordon, our commentator on this passage, touches on our own despair at "the death sentence of causality." Some things just don't work out the way we want. Jesus, himself, rails against the fact that not everything turns out well. Jim Macy, our group leader, told us last week that it's helpful to see Jesus as Everyman. ("If we see him as Superman," he said, "we might as well just go back to reading Marvel comics.")

Maggie challenges us to be that Everyman, to get past the deficiencies others may have. What a great way to help me get beyond the metric of keeping score of gifts and expressions of thanks!

— Felix

NOVEMBER 25, 2010

Dear Family,

This is the morning of Thanksgiving Day here in the USA. Before accusing me of proclaiming the obvious, I want you to know that this letter now goes to Maggie's nieces and nephews in Australia. As my niece, Rose Grayson, mentioned recently, an unexpected outcome of these letters is that they have helped us to come together as an extended family. I've added a photo of Andrew McGown and his wife, Robyn, taken in Bali in 2008, to the photo album. One glance, and I know we are all reassured that there will be no degradation of the gene pool. What an attractive couple!

This is the most universal of American holidays, but Thanksgiving always seemed to have a unique Rogerian aspect when I was in high school. I remember the huge platter that Maggie used when she served dinner; it had so many turkey motifs its use was pre-ordained. She did have one unusual food favorite: rutabagas. Despite our complaints about their bitter taste, they always made their way to the Thanksgiving feast. Perhaps to prove she always had the upper hand, one year our centerpiece was a huge waxed rutabaga, surrounded by garnishes of cabbage leaves and other ornaments. I don't want to let these reminiscences prove that I have such a good memory that I now recall things that never happened, so I'll ask of my siblings: I remember how rich her turkey stuffing was. Did she add oysters to it?

Dad's participation was inconsistent, since this was the era before he discovered that there was a kitchen in the house. Some years, he ordered a Smithfield ham to go with the turkey. If you are unfamiliar with it, think of fine Corinthian leather. They tell me that the leather is equally tender, but not nearly as salty. During his gadget years, his contribution was to unpack the electric knife and carve the turkey with a surgical flourish, making sure that the long electric cord didn't knock over a wineglass as he disarticulated the drumstick.

Maggie and Dad were at the office yesterday. Dad brought by the organic turkey that will be part of their dinner with Valerie Overholt and her family. I delivered it to her last night. He turned down dinner invitations from Jody and me because it is "tradition" to join Valerie.

At the office, Maggie was wearing a lovely tweed jacket. Despite her perfect posture and very straight shoulders, she has become so diminutive that she barely looked like she belonged in it. We wished each other a happy Thanksgiving. Her eyes were so bright and her smile so endearing that a lump immediately rose in my throat. I continue to be enchanted by Maggie's loving demeanor and serenity. I know it may just be the type of dementia she has, but, perhaps it reflects her core personality.

On a day like this, with no need to leave immediately for work, I enjoy contemplative reading. The idea of giving thanks seems to be part of nearly all value systems, so today I went to the source document for my faith tradition, where the phrase completes a three-part injunction: "Rejoice always, pray without ceasing, give thanks in all circumstances." (1 Thessalonians 5:16-18, NRSV)[10]

For those of you for whom the personal journey doesn't have a religious aspect, bear with me for a moment. I know the stumbling block is to "pray without ceasing." I recall that my sister Sheila and I wrestled with this in high school when we read "Franny and Zooey" by J.D. Salinger.[11] It seemed improbable and impractical. I can't imagine telling the family of a patient that their relative died because I was saying prayers continually and didn't have time to pay attention to the problem!

By good fortune, my daily reading today of John Main, the Roman Catholic priest and Benedictine monk who presented a way of Christian meditation, addressed this topic.[12] His method of prayer involves a mantra, which "keeps guard" over the heart so extraneous trivia does not enter in, not "even our own pious, holy words and thoughts." Praying without ceasing is not saying a steady stream of words. Rather, it is our continuous attention to keep guard over the heart. And what is our attention protecting? Why, our rejoicing and thanksgiving, of course!

Back to Maggie. Today I see her as completely untainted by trivia. It may be an aspect of intellectual snobbery that we don't honor simplicity and purity. It is so customary to value nuance and articulate speech that true expressions of the heart may go unnoticed. Fortunately, since she is my mom, I am compelled to honor her expressions of the true heart.

My hope is to extend this honor to all in my circle — especially in case someone might try to serve me rutabaga today!

— Felix

DECEMBER 5, 2010

Dear Family,

Sometimes small gestures convey a lot of meaning. For example, Dad has always held out the chair for Maggie when she sits down at dinner. Earlier this week, Maggie was a bit more confused than usual as we were getting ready for dinner. She kept saying that she needed to round everybody up, and then she left to look for them. Maybe holding the chair out was part of a familiar routine that helped center her thoughts because she stopped asking about the rest of the family as soon as it was held out for her and she sat down.

This weekend, I bumped into a person I've known since elementary school. I was surprised by her statement: "The difference between you and me was parenting. You had great parenting, and I didn't have any."

I didn't pursue which aspects of parenting she had in mind. But I do recall that polite behavior was one thing on which we were coached, both with instruction and with role models.

Why are we taught manners, or any other behavior, for that matter? The obvious answer is so we are able to implement that behavior when the situation calls for it, just as a vaccination prepares the immune system for an event that may not occur until years later. The trick is to recognize the situation and then respond properly. I know there have been many times when an event has come and gone before I realized what was called for.

Earlier this week, my sister Sheila wrote with her concern that my initial Maggie Letters were harsh in my description of our father's response to Maggie's broken elbow. As I recall things, we were all concerned about some aspects of his actions and worried that he wasn't grasping key elements of the situation. Now I see that's understandable. After all, this was the first time he'd had to confront the situation of a sudden injury to Maggie. As I look back on the events, it's pretty dramatic to see how he gained control of things and how remarkably well everything is going now.

It's also clear that this was my first chance to be the son pushed into the role of supportive caregiver. In retrospect, I didn't do as well as I could have at the time.

Maggie is completing one of the last milestones in the life journey. As I look at my own life milestones — the first day of school, high school graduation, college, marriage, children — I note that these events have sharp edges, and the timetable is pretty much expected. In contrast, Maggie's cognitive decline may have been going on for a few years before it was really noticed, and it's only been a recent development that it has become the defining feature of her health. (As Sheila wrote to me, "dementia" is much harsher than the term "cognitive decline," and the latter is more descriptive of the clinical time course.) Our society now accepts the idea that advertisements need to have a bite, an edge. But Maggie's condition and Sheila's admonition make it clear that these are times for soft edges and smoothing out of the rough spots. Just accepting this to be true has a calming influence on me.

We four Rogers kids have been the recipients of a wonderful legacy of parenting. Some of the lessons were simple, like having good manners and being polite, especially to older people. Others were life skills that we integrated into our personality, so we may draw on them for unexpected events that arise. These Maggie Letters have given me a good chance to examine how well I am doing with these challenges, and I appreciate the feedback I have received.

— Felix

DECEMBER 18, 2010

Dear Family,

I stopped by the holiday dinner celebration for the Downriver Reversal Team on Tuesday night. My brother Jody started this group around 1991 as a way to halt or reverse coronary artery disease without medications, relying instead on a plant-based, ultra low-fat diet, exercise and yoga. This approach was based on the work of Dean Ornish,[13] which Jody introduced to our patients shortly before statin drugs became available. A person at the table where I was seated pointed out that her mother had memory problems. "But she still remembers my name, so it's not 'Alt Heimer's.'" The members of the group are a remarkably healthy-looking group of people, but their understanding, and pronunciation, of Alzheimer's disease is pretty basic.

I recently realized that I have been engaged in uncharacteristic behavior, at least for me, in these letters. I haven't said a thing about the mechanisms of Alzheimer's disease or any other dementia. Generally, I feel most comfortable if I can identify information about the things around me, whether in the plant, animal or mineral realm. Over the years, I've worn out a lot of people with my recitation of facts.

The *Science* section of *The New York Times* on December 14, 2010, had a feature article about Alzheimer's.[14] The article made me grateful for the skills of a good science writer. This reporter, Gina Kolata, did a masterful job of delving into the new research on the topic. I'd like to share with you some of what she wrote.

The first important issue in the cause of Alzheimer's disease is beta amyloid, a protein originally thought to cause the disease because of its apparent overproduction in patients. The new insight is that it is probably produced in normal amounts in Alzheimer's patients, and a delayed elimination of the protein is the culprit instead.[15] Beta amyloid is a normal compound in the brain and, in small quantities, probably serves to control signaling between cells. However, when it accumulates, nerve impulses may stop altogether, nerves can die, and the disease takes hold.

I think the most interesting aspect of the new research is the back story. Where does Alzheimer's attack the brain, and is there anything to do about it? *The New York Times* article introduced me to the "default system of the brain," a system of cells that is always turned on at some level. It includes the brain's memory center (the hippocampus), and it is the brain's mind-wandering mode, the part that is active when we daydream about something while performing a task, such as driving a car.

The increased levels of beta amyloid seem to preferentially attack the default network. Besides daydreaming and memory, the default system is used in our sense of self. If a person is asked if a list of adjectives — such as, honest, kind and thoughtful — reflects the way he thinks, he uses his default network to determine if this is accurate about himself.

Since only the default network is under attack in a patient with Alzheimer's, this fact may lead to clues to help treat the disease. The less active the brain — such as after a stroke or a closed- head injury — the less beta amyloid is made. During sleep, the default system is less active and, perhaps, less amyloid is made. If so, sleep-deprived people might be at greater risk of Alzheimer's disease; this is now a subject of research.

On the other hand, people with more education are less prone to Alzheimer's. The researchers hypothesize that education, by encouraging more deliberate problem solving and thought, decreases the activity of the default network.

I can't resist some conjecture based on this information. Maggie has always complained about lack of sleep. But no one would ever accuse her of excessive daydreaming and lack of focused thought. And, I wonder, going beyond Maggie's case, would a mindfulness practice or the type of meditation the Dalai Lama describes as "calm abiding"[16] represent the type of focused activity that inhibits amyloid production? We have research on the risk for Alzheimer's disease in nuns (lower word count—a surrogate for IQ—on their convent entrance essay was a marker of increased risk), but what do we know about Alzheimer's in people who meditate?

It's also interesting that the default system is the most metabolically active part of the brain, using huge amounts of glucose. Low glucose uptake by the brain is a sign of Alzheimer's disease. Do we feel tired after daydreaming? Isn't it true that when we are in the "flow," time just flies by?

How is our sense of self implicated in Alzheimer's? I've been fascinated by Maggie's unfettered demeanor and a heart uncluttered by trivia. Is that just a biochemical feature of the disease, or is this her true personality coming to the fore?

— Felix

DECEMBER 20, 2010

Dear Family,

I stood before the front door of my parents' house Sunday and looked down at the basket in my arms. I had put together a Christmas gift basket. Everything was organic, of course. I had dried Turkish figs and apricots, Medjool dates, walnuts and fresh roasted macadamia nuts, and lots of fruit. It all looked pretty pathetic. Caroline had helped me arrange the things, placing cellophane "grass" around the larger items and tying ribbons around the packets of fruit. Otherwise, I think it would have looked like I was carrying something intended to go directly to the compost heap.

I remembered the gifts we always made Maggie when we were so young. Sheila and Lisa made potholders from little kits. One year Jody and I made birdhouses. He was much better with his hands than I, and his even looked a bit like a birdhouse. Mine was so lopsided that it wouldn't stand up, and it proved too crooked to be nailed to a tree.

The following year, we all made her potholders. She was such a good sport, carrying on about how skillful we all were.

That may have been the same year we all got "Indian sweaters." I think they were from British Columbia, and the folks each had one, too. They were distinctive, made from thick wool rich with lanolin, with interesting patterns and designs. I imagine that we made quite a statement when we all went out together.

This picture must have been taken by Maggie at Mesa Verde, Arizona, about 1954. It shows us in our "Indian Sweaters."

On this Sunday, Dad and Maggie helped me into the house. Together we opened up the basket, and I talked about the contents. I think Dad was especially glad to get the six frozen, gluten-free organic entrees I also had brought along.

Dad then showed me the things that he had bought for Caroline and me, and our daughters and their husbands. It was a striking collection: dates, cheese, nuts and crackers. Much the same items I had given them. It is remarkable that he had the time to do this in addition to his work and caring for Maggie.

After exchanging our gifts, we sat down to the lunch that Dad had prepared, a chicken soup. Ever the student, he asked some basic questions about making stock from scratch versus the store-bought kind. While we ate, he reminded me of the episode when Maggie and her best friend and neighbor, Vivian Overholt, went shopping in downtown Detroit.

They found a 10-inch frosted-glass statue of the Madonna that rested on a base, which lit up, sending a warm glow through the entire statue. It was very expensive, and they agreed that it was out of their price range. The next day, each of them called the store and asked for the statue to be held on layaway. Months later, on Christmas Day, Maggie and Vivian opened the gifts that were too expensive for either to buy for herself but perfect to give a best friend. They were each bowled over by thoughtfulness of the other, and displayed their own frosted-glass statue of the Madonna with special affection.

I had to see patients at the hospital before I joined my parents for lunch. Ever since reading about the effects of Alzheimer's on the default network of the brain, I've been thinking about the other aspects of Alzheimer's in addition to memory loss, especially the loss of recognition of self. At the hospital this day, I saw a patient whose story now made more sense to me than it might have otherwise. Let's say his name was Cliff. He had symptoms that were not typical for cardiac pain, and I asked if it might be stress. When I asked about his source of stress, he told me that his wife had Alzheimer's. Cliff said there were things about his wife's condition that were funny and others that tore at his heart. The other day he came home and heard laughter from his wife's room. There she was, pointing at her reflection in the mirror and saying, "Look at my sister Theresa! She's wearing exactly the same shirt that I am."

Then he told me about his admission to the hospital the previous day. He came to the emergency room in the afternoon, but didn't get to his hospital bed until 2 a.m. He called his daughter to tell her his room number, and she said that his wife wanted to wish him good night. Cliff's eyes welled up with tears as he told me about this. Then he added, "The hard thing is that I know that she loves me, but she has no way of understanding my emotional needs, or the things that bother me."

Now at lunch with my folks, I had to get up from the lunch table to answer a call from the hospital, and as I did, I watched Maggie lean across the table and ask, "Joe, did you get enough lunch? Can I get you anything more?"

— Felix

CHAPTER FOUR

Exploring How the Brain Works

JANUARY 1, 2011

Dear Family,

A couple decades ago, I had dinner with James Schoenberger, M.D., who was then the immediate past president of the American Heart Association. He is imbued with charm and leads the conversation smoothly. Still, I felt the need to add something, so I asked him what he was going to do in his free time now that his term with the AHA had ended. He said that he was going to find the cure for Alzheimer's disease.

Now, he is a world-famous researcher, but I couldn't help asking what he knew about Alzheimer's that would allow him to make such a bold statement. He said he knew almost nothing about the disease itself, but he did know that it was a problem of great public health proportions, so the first step would be to learn the epidemiology of the problem. That's what he had done with heart disease. He envisioned the research would be pretty straightforward from there.

Armed with the same confidence, I decided that I would take the Christmas weekend to search the literature and learn the current understanding of the causes and treatment of Alzheimer's disease. It's so rare for me to have unprogrammed time. I should have been able to accomplish that and more in the three-day weekend.

After two days of research, I felt pretty confident: I had a cohesive data set that made a lot of sense to me. The next day, I checked on one more aspect of the information I had, and my balloon burst. I'd like to list all of the information I had gathered up to this point, but it wouldn't do any good, except perhaps to assuage my sense of time ill-spent.

The bottom line is that nature has provided us with multiple redundant systems in just about every aspect of what we do. For example, we don't have just one chemical that controls blood pressure. We have at least five or six. Likewise, the brain has multiple areas that are involved in memory. And in each area, there are multiple nerve connections, each with multiple neurotransmitters, and multiple proteins and enzymes that control their function. At the moment, there are lots of promising areas of study, but the unifying data just aren't there.

I will comment on a few things. One is how the beta-amyloid plaque does its damage. An amyloid precursor protein stabilizes the synapse, the communication space between nerves. When this connection isn't used, or isn't necessary, the amyloid precursor protein is broken into fragments, one of which is beta amyloid. When these beta amyloid particles accumulate, they cause damage to the brain, especially the areas of the default brain, which includes those areas associated with memory. Several compounds have been identified which increase the risk of the buildup of beta amyloid. Likewise, there are several promising substances that may retard or even reverse this process.

At the present time, I think there are a few approaches to the prevention of Alzheimer's disease. Besides these incompletely defined molecular mechanisms, we know the same things that cause hardening of the arteries cause Alzheimer's: smoking, being overweight, the lack of exercise, high blood cholesterol, high blood pressure and diabetes.

What interests me the most is the idea that the amyloid precursor protein is broken down into its toxic components when the nerve connections in the brain are no longer functioning. It raises the specter of, "If you don't use it, you lose it." And, if that is true, are there things we should be doing to exercise our brain to minimize the chance of this happening? In today's New York Times, Oliver Sacks, our pre-eminent commentator on the brain, advocated a New Year's resolution for the brain,[18] not just the usual pledge to make this the year to implement an exercise program. I found it conspicuous that he didn't comment on any exercises to prevent Alzheimer's, although it seems so logical.

Since one way to control nerve traffic is meditation, I also conducted a search of that topic this past weekend. Here, too, the literature has mixed results. I'll address these findings in a subsequent letter.

By good luck, today's Times also had an article on care of patients with Alzheimer's.[19] The important point is that personal care of the patient and support of the caregiver is the most useful aspect of treatment at this time since we don't have effective medications. It's this component where we can feel most comfortable with Maggie's care, since Dad is doing such a remarkable job with her. However, there are still areas of concern. As Lisa and I commented during our visit today, lighting plays a part in the treatment of this disease, and the folks have dismal lighting. Also, the *Times* emphasized the need to give patients what they want, even if it's chocolate! That's not going to happen in the Rogers' house, since Dad now feels that sugar is a major culprit in many of the diseases of our modern culture. He's probably right.

I'll close with an interesting exchange. Maggie was laughing and in good spirits. I asked about her dinner with Jody earlier this week:

"I hear you had a great lobster dinner with Jody."

"I did?"

"Yes. He said you really dug into your lobster."

"Oh, that's good. I was afraid you were going to say something unusual."

This sort of baffling exchange has become a familiar element in our conversations. As people with Alzheimer's disease progress in their cognitive decline, they sometimes maintain fluency in their speech, but the logic and the associations break down.[20] Sometimes the linkages are funny, the way a typo in a letter can trip you up. There is also sadness in these, because it is the foreboding of further decline.

— Felix

JANUARY 8, 2011

Dear Family,

My spirits sagged today, as I looked at all the titles relating to Alzheimer's disease. Borders bookstore has a full shelf devoted to the topic. I found my enthusiasm waning, in part, because this excursion into the science behind Alzheimer's is taking up so much time. Out of a sense of duty, I bought a book on the care of a family member with Alzheimer's.[21]

I think that the strength of these letters comes from my personal perspective on Maggie. I recall when I read a lot of Elie Wiesel 20 years ago that I found his reflections on the intersection of existentialism and Orthodox Judaism to be interesting, but my real fascination was with his stories of the people in the Holocaust.

So, I'll just tell you what's on my mind (pun not intended) and then get back to Maggie.

I continue to ponder this issue of the default brain, the part of our brain that is continuously active and which controls memory, daydreaming and our sense of self. I really only know enough to be dangerous, so I welcome comments from readers.

I am particularly interested in these three issues:

First of all, although the term may be new, the "default brain" may well be addressed in the first sentence of the Yoga Sutra: "Yoga is the suppression of the oscillations of the mental substance." This has been attributed to Patanjali, which places its origin in the second century BCE. Some feel the idea may be even older. Either way, this idea of a part of the brain that never shuts down (i.e., the oscillations) seems to be a part of ancient wisdom.

The next issue is the role of the default brain in Alzheimer's. The literature is clear that the default brain is the area attacked by the beta amyloid plaque, which causes the disease. There is evidence that the default brain functions abnormally in early Alzheimer's, becoming more active when normally it would be inhibited. There are inferences that inappropriate activity of the default brain — as with sleep deprivation — may be causative in the disease process.

Finally: Yet, a key portion of the disease process is that beta amyloid fragments are produced when synapses no longer fire, and the amyloid precursor protein is broken down ("If you don't use it, you lose it."). On the surface, it can't be both ways: that over-activity of the default brain leads to Alzheimer's, and that the lack of use of the same brain areas causes production of beta amyloid.

I can only make sense of this in one way. One component of the scientific community feels that the default brain is always active in order to maintain the brain in a state of readiness. The other camp holds that the mind wanders simply because it can. We know the other component of the brain, the executive brain, suppresses the default brain. My supposition is that the healthy brain has a balance between suppression of the oscillations of the default brain to learn a new task, for example, and dynamic activity of the default brain during memory recall, creative thinking and dreaming sleep.

By analogy, the healthy state for the cardiovascular system is when there is the greatest variability of the normal heartbeat, not a precisely regular pulse. Likewise, athletes train for distance running by doing interval work, fast-paced activity interspersed with a less-demanding pace. We enjoy tension and release in most of the creative things we do, including music and other things that affect our emotional life.

I'm savvy enough not to address my last topic, which is a more ontological question. Where does the person reside in the brain? The default brain is involved in our sense of self, but is that where the "I" lives? I've grappled with the medical and religious literature on this topic for a few years now, and I'll save it for another time.

In the next letter, I'll be back to Maggie and her singing.

— Felix

JANUARY 11, 2011

Dear Family,

I know I shouldn't be so concerned about my credentials for writing a blog, but you should, perhaps, know that I flunked Marijuana 101. Twice. The first occasion was when I was a junior in college and my roommate, now a distinguished emergency medicine physician in Maine, brought some weed for us to share in our dorm room. Like many of my patients who are given a prescription medication, I got all of the adverse side effects and none of the advertised benefits.

Felix with Mickey,
Kirksville, Missouri, 1971

My second chance for this socially necessary rite came my second year of medical school. My roommate, Mickey, had transferred from Kirksville to the University of Minnesota School of Medicine. He invited me up for the weekend. Mickey had tickets to see Livingston Taylor, the younger brother of James. He also had some "regulation roach clips" from a senior student in medical school — hemostats from the operating room — which allowed us to keep our fingers cool as we smoked the joint down to the embers, but we still burned our lips. We had a joint in his apartment, another in the car, and I think we even smoked one in the lobby of the Guthrie Theater. This time social isolation and sadness overpowered the dry mouth and dizzy sensation.

My transcript for this life experience is forever stuck at 0-2, since I'm not willing to take a makeup exam.

This second episode makes me wonder if I also failed Basic Childhood Experiences. Livingston Taylor was enjoyable, and we had great seats, but the concert seemed uninspired to me until he sang "Somewhere Over the Rainbow." The audience went nuts, and I wondered how so many people could know a song that to my knowledge was something only sung by Maggie when she worked in the kitchen. I was lucky to keep my thoughts to myself as we headed to the exits, and I overheard someone make a comment about "The Wizard of Oz." I didn't let Mickey know that our childhood TV time was so restricted that I had made it this far in life without seeing the movie from start to finish.

Another of these songs Maggie sang in our childhood came back with special poignancy this weekend. Saturday was Alison's 30th birthday, and her husband, Randy Napoleon, was performing with his ensemble at Detroit's top jazz restaurant, the Dirty Dog. It was a wonderful evening. On my right were our best friends, Alan and Sharon Hoffman; our daughter Beth sat on my left with her husband, Jim. Caroline was across the table sitting next to Emily Austin, Alison's best friend for her whole life. Emily is so darling that she even looked cute as she grimaced when the waiter handed her a hot platter of lobster risotto. When the group played "All the Way" ("When somebody loves you, it's no good unless they love you"), I simultaneously took in this present family moment and recalled the many times I had heard Maggie sing that around the house. I got a lump in my throat, big time, which I tried to diminish by asking Jim to take some photos.

The remarkable thing is that Maggie still sings on occasion. In September, we took our annual trip to our vacation spot in northern Ontario. It's such a long trip that Caroline and I take lots of CDs to listen to in the car, especially since Maggie likes music so much. When Chanticleer sang "Danny Boy" or "Loch Lomond," Maggie sang right along. Her pitch was true, and she remembered all the words. We played these pieces disproportionately and would have played them many times more, except that we were so moved by the endearing sweetness of the event, it seemed we were overdoing it.

All my reading on Alzheimer's does nothing to explain this sort of thing. How is it that her memory is intact for music, but there are days she doesn't know who I am? Isn't it strange that a few years ago, all the fascination was about left brain-right brain, and now it's about the executive brain and the default brain? Isn't it typical that we always try to make things clear-cut, sometimes at the expense of facts, just to feel that we understand something?

Perhaps I am drawn to explore the analyses of the mechanics of the mind, just as other members of our society are attracted to experiment with marijuana and the manipulation of the mind.

— Felix

JANUARY 28, 2011

Dear Family,

I have received requests from Alison and Rose to comment on my earlier posts about how meditation works in the brain. It's taken me a while to read enough that I think I can elaborate on my previous statements. The literature is complex and dense. Space does not allow me to comment on the research on both of the two major types of meditation, focused attention and open monitoring. Instead, I will comment on mindfulness, one type of open monitoring. With this, I hope to address those aspects of brain function that play a major part in our daily lives and which are affected by Alzheimer's disease.

The starting point is to consider the brain in terms of memory and our sense of self. Both are areas severely affected by Alzheimer's disease. Although the idea of self has been explored in literature for more than 2,000 years, current research starts with references to William James. In 1890, he characterized the "self" as a "source of permanence beneath the constantly shifting set of experiences that constitute conscious life."[22] The permanent aspect of this requires our memory to be a construction of narratives that bind our past experiences into a cohesive fabric. (The choice of the word "narratives" will become clearer soon.) James felt that our continuity could be understood in terms of an explanatory "me" that makes sense of the "I" acting in the present moment.

Usually, we identify ourselves by telling a story about who we are. For example: I was born in Washington, D.C., and moved to Detroit when I was very little. I graduated from high school while living Downriver, and I still work in the area. I'm married, I have children, and I am a die-hard Detroit Tigers baseball fan (as long as they are winning).

I have a great job, and I really enjoy the work that I do. Just about everybody that I work with is great, except this one person. It seems as if all I need to do is say one wrong thing, and the whole day is shot, and I can't do anything right. (This example is intended to show how the narrative self can get carried away when it runs with an idea.)

When we describe who we are by making it part of a story, like the example above, our description involves our narrative self. Another such example would be what we put on a resume or a job application.

The other way we can say who we are is to put things in specific terms to describe ourselves in this exact moment. For example: I am here. I'm sitting in a room with a lot of strangers. I'm feeling a little shy. The room is just a little too warm, and I have a knot in my left shoulder muscle, close to my neck. The person next to me is sending text messages on his cell phone. I'm trying to breathe slowly in order to relax some.

When we describe ourselves in terms of what we are noticing about our personal situation, what we are experiencing at this moment, we are referring to the experiential self.

Brain imaging studies that use functional magnetic resonance imaging (fMRI) can now map the brain regions involved in each of these aspects of self, the narrative and the experiential focus, the latter representing the "I" in the present moment, the "I am here." Functional MRI involves the use of magnets in a machine, similar to a CT scan, to image the brain based on the blood flow and oxygen levels in specific regions. The idea is that when we use certain regions of the brain, more blood flow is delivered to those areas to allow greater oxygen uptake, and the machine is able to record these changes based on electromagnetic changes on a cellular level.

The "me," or narrative self, which includes our memories, is located in the front part of the brain near the central area, which is called the midline. This area of the brain is named the medial prefrontal cortex (mPFC), and it actually includes several brain areas, as you will see shortly. The mPFC has been shown to support a variety of self-related capacities, including memory for self-traits, reflected self-knowledge and aspirations for the future. In other words, these midline cortical areas support narrative references to our sense of who we are, which allows us to maintain continuity of self over time. The narrative self is the part of us who keeps track of and tells the "story" of our life.

The "experiential" sense of momentary self-reference is quite different. For one thing, it may represent core aspects of self-experience achieved earlier in development. Little is known about the neural markers for momentary self-reference. The brain area involved may be based on transient body states, such as those due to sensation of outside events by our body and its sensing organs, and the sensing of states within our body, such as breathing. We tap into this when we do yoga or relaxation techniques, and the leader asks us to be aware of our bodies — to notice the weight of our sitting bones on the chair, to feel our diaphragm move as we breathe, and so forth. The anatomic "home" for the part of the brain that records our awareness of ourselves as we notice these things appears to be in the lateral parts of the brain, especially the right insular cortex. (Please see the top figure on page 108.)

How these areas are affected by our thoughts was tested in a series of ingenious experiments at the University of Toronto and Atlanta's Emory University, where subjects were given a value-laden adjective, like "confident" or "melancholy."

To define the narrative focus, the subjects were asked to judge what was happening in their brain when they thought about the adjective, figure out what that trait word meant to them, and whether it described them or not. Also during the interview, they were allowed to get carried away and follow any train of thought that occurred.

In contrast, to define the experiential focus, subjects were asked to focus on their current body state without purpose or goal, other than noticing how things were from one moment to the next. They were instructed to ignore the trait adjectives, other than to notice that a word had been used. If they found their mind wandering, they were asked to calmly return their attention to their current experiences.

Functional magnetic imaging was used to define a baseline value for each subject. The volunteers were then randomized into two groups, one of which received an eight-week training program of mindfulness meditation (following the method practiced by Jon Kabat-Zinn) to enhance their ability to stay present in the moment. These subjects were retested after the training period. (Please see the lower figure on page 108.)

The narrative focus plays a major role in psychology and mental health. Mood and anxiety disorders lie in these same brain areas, and the narrative focus increases our vulnerability to illness. My cousin Jamie, a psychologist visiting from Australia this weekend, tells me that this information is used in cognitive psychology, as in, "This narrative is your story. It is under your control. You can change it."

The experiential focus shifts our thoughts away from the areas of affective response to a more self-detached and objective analysis of sensory events. This allows us to separate the affective and sensory aspects of pain, in other words, to reduce the suffering associated with pain. For this reason, mindfulness meditation has been shown to have clinical utility in the management of chronic pain.

The important question for me is whether this idea of self can help us understand ourselves? On the spiritual journey, we are told to leave the self behind. By tradition, we interpret this to mean to leave behind the false self, the ego. I think the research helps us to understand that there is nothing intrinsically wrong with the narrative self. The problem is daydreaming, which introduces all manner of false images, thoughts and emotions. What do we have left when the narrative focus is appropriately suppressed by attention in the moment or by focused attention on a particular object?

I don't often read Jiddu Krishnamurti (1895-1986), but I turned to his daily meditation for January 28.[23] He seems to indicate that approaching life without the bias inherent in our memories is the best way to see reality as it is:

> "It is important to understand what this self-knowing is, just to be aware, without any choice, of the 'me' which has its source in a bundle of memories — just to be conscious of it without interpretation, merely to observe the movement of the mind … That is, I have to observe and see the fact, the actual, the 'what is.' If I approach it with an idea, with an opinion, such as 'I must not,' or 'I must,' which are responses of memory, then the movement of what is hindered is blocked; and, therefore, there is no learning."

— Felix

FEBRUARY 1, 2011

Dear Family,

Today is the 67th wedding anniversary of Joseph Trivilla Rogers and Sheila Mabel McGown Rogers (aka, Maggie).

The celebration has been modest. In Rogerian fashion, we had planned to hold a short celebration of this as part of our mini-family reunion with my cousin Jamie Jackson on this past Saturday. Unfortunately, Dad was ill, and he and Maggie were unable to make it up to our house. We had purchased some special items for appetizers: bosterma (a smelly Armenian cured tenderloin steak with paprika), and three cheeses to accompany it (kashkaval, Greek feta, and another sliced cheese that the butcher recommended), since all of his friends liked it so much!

Even though our parents missed the party, the rest of us sampled the bosterma and cheese with our champagne, and I took the leftovers to work yesterday. Maggie and Dad arrived at work about 10 a.m. Maggie was wearing the brushed mohair coat that she knitted years ago and kept her thick wool gloves on. She didn't remember the phone conversation she had with Jamie two days before. Maggie got her infusion of megavitamins with hopes to ward off further incursions of beta amyloid, and Dad went off to see his morning patients.

When I saw Dad today, he said the food we had brought over was so good that he and Maggie had it for dinner last night. It reminded me of Caroline's grandmother Mamie, who, at age 95, could make a dinner out of Triscuits, cheese and a glass of sherry. There is an upside to the decline of metabolism with age.

I am reminded that we had a great party for the folks on their 50th anniversary. Dad opened a bottle of sherry from 1899 that his friend Muzzy bought at an estate sale in Toledo. He told a cute story of the man who had trouble convincing his wife they should buy some expensive champagne. He won her over only by promising that it could be great at a special celebration. When their own golden wedding anniversary arrived, she noticed the bottles still up on the shelf. After she pointed that out, he said, "Oh, that. I'm saving it for a really special time." Dad did agree, on their 50th, that this event merited the bottle of 95-year-old sherry.

When Jamie was here, we tossed around the idea of dysfunctional family life. As I look back on our efforts to celebrate a family event, the first temptation was to consider this a mark of a dysfunctional state. In defense of celebrating an anniversary over the course of four days, in two locations and with leftovers rather than a banquet, we did have the disadvantage of illness on Grosse Ile, ice storms in Cleveland that delayed Lisa's arrival and full office schedules for all three Rogers boys. Sometimes that's just the way things turn out.

Speaking of dysfunctional, I'm at the age when emotions bubble up unexpectedly. At dinner, my son-in-law, the priest, begged off on saying grace. As I ad-libbed something about being thankful for the gift of the family together, I was surprised by a sudden choke in my throat. To add insult to injury, a letter from my college roommate yesterday accused me of being a romantic! So, I'm treading softly on these anniversary issues and even harboring a secret satisfaction in getting to be in closer touch with my more emotional side.

Meanwhile, on Saturday, Jody and I were enjoying bosterma here in Pleasant Ridge and trying to get Jamie and the rest of the family to try it. (It is awfully smelly — authentic "guy" food). The other trick was to eat it and not get any fingerprints on the shoebox full of old photos that Jody and Rosemary had brought up with them. Jody and Jamie found a lot, which will appear in "The Maggie Letters" over the next few weeks. I also want to get the photos into the genealogy album that I would like to develop with support from all of you. Searching through all these boxes, I found my journal from our trip to Australia in 1961, and Lisa wrote to me that she found hers, too. Considering that I was 14, it's not too bad, but I got behind, and there are no entries for Australia!

I'll conclude this note with photos we found from that trip.

— Felix

Top Left: Aden, Yemen, July 1961; Top Right: Stonehenge, June, 1961
Bottom Left: Waiting for traffic to clear, near Penang, Malasia, July, 1961
Bottom Right: Maggie & JTR at York Minster, England, June 20, 1961. Lisa is on the right.

Left: Australia, 1961;
Top Right: Jody holds a koala bear cub, near Melbourne, Australia, August, 1961
Bottom Right: Hong Kong/Kowloon Harbor, August, 1961

FEBRUARY 27, 2011

Dear Family,

This is the type of day that tests the resiliency of a Michigan native. The sun hasn't been out for five or six days, we've had lots of snow and it's been just warm enough that we have piles of dirty grime on the sides of the roads. To add to it all, today is especially foggy. I can barely see across the river, and Canada is faint and indistinct on the horizon. I am sitting with my parents at tea, well past the defined 4 o'clock hour because of my schedule at work, but too early to have dinner. Dad was pleased to use his new, bright yellow teapot, which he bought from a catalogue.

Maggie always adds a comment about the view from their living room. They have a large picture window and sweeping views of the Detroit River, with the skyline of Detroit to the north, Canada directly to the east and a collection of small islands to the south, with Jody and Rosemary's boat dock in the foreground. Today there are just a few swans and Canada geese on the river. A small flock of bufflehead ducks bob in the water for a while before moving on. It's gray, river to sky, but it's also quiet and peaceful.

Sheila and Lisa wrote to me after their visit here last weekend. They both had a tough time. Not only did Sheila get snowed in and have her flight canceled, leading to a two-day delay, but I had assigned her the task of following up on my conversation with Dad about hearing aids. As a testament to how much he needs them, we talked by telephone while she was at the folks' house. I'm sure that Sheila was in a location we otherwise would have characterized as "within hearing distance." It sounded as if it had been an unpleasant conversation, with Dad not only rejecting the idea, but also rejecting the concept that family members and friends were entitled to offer him such suggestions. He was prickly, to say the least. Whereas he hadn't been thrilled with my conversations about hearing aids the week before, his response seemed much more harsh, probably because he may feel threatened or boxed in if he gets too many suggestions in a short period of time.

Today, the conversation went back and forth as usual. I try to direct as much talk as I can to Maggie, knowing that she enjoys the attention and is glad not to feel obligated to initiate a new topic or expand on something that I say. When I want to include Dad in the conversation, I look directly at him, speak slowly and raise my voice 50 decibels. Today he wanted to lead the conversation. He gave me a nod that indicated my need to pay attention, as he addressed the issue of the relation between the phases of the moon and earthquakes. He enjoys holding an advantage over me on this one. Years ago, we were in Petoskey, Michigan, about four hours north of Detroit. It was a clear night with a full moon as we walked back from dinner. He commented on the likelihood of an earthquake in the next day or so. The following Monday, there was a newspaper clipping on my desk about the quake that occurred shortly after our conversation.

He paused to emphasize the certainty of his remarks, as he alluded to the quake in New Zealand last month. I didn't bother to ask if it occurred during a full moon. I talked for a short time and probably made something up about plate tectonics and the putative depth of influence that the moon might have on the earth's crust. Brushing that aside, he added that on March 19, the Farmer's Almanac is calling for record tides as well. He suggested that I mark my calendar. You, my readers, have heard it here first.

Lisa's plaint was more poignant and may have no solution. She wrote to say she was in tears as she drove back to Cleveland, shocked by how much Maggie has slipped and saddened that she has lost her mother. She asked me to write something inspirational in the next Maggie Letter.

That's no small task, but I can provide what I do to cope with the emotional burden, something that was re-enforced recently by my reading of a new book on Alzheimer's patients ("A Caregiver's Guide to Alzheimer's Disease," by Patricia Callone, et al.[20]) The experts recommend that we don't spend time mourning what has been lost, but we focus on what remains. This book, to which I will refer more later, gives great hints about how we might focus on the enduring and charming potential of the patient with early Alzheimer's. Maggie is now in middle to later stages of the disease, so some of the amusing anecdotes in this book are enticing, but less apropos.

I do ascribe to the advice to center on those traits that remain. I cherish Maggie's sweet demeanor, her kindness and her ready sense of humor. We laugh a lot together. But, as these letters attest, I also spend a good deal of time remembering Maggie and our family in our best times.

Here's my rationale, based on a story I've told so many times I no longer remember if it happened, but I know it's true. A patient was in tears talking about her husband's death years ago. Then she told me how a friend told her to look at these moments in a different way. Each time she was moved to tears about her husband's death, she was to remind herself that she thought of him because of her steadfast love for him. This allowed her to remember the adage that love is stronger than death. Her love did persist far beyond the grave.

Maggie is still with us, in many ways. But the Maggie we loved as children and young adults has been gone for some time. I am not letting go of my love just yet. My reflections on her role in our lives helps to keep alive her vibrant, full personality that was such a strong force for so many of us.

— Felix

MARCH 8, 2011

Dear Family,

I'm now halfway through my second book about Alzheimer's disease. Unlike the first, which was centered on understanding the person in terms of the neurological changes involved in each stage of the disease, this one ("Learning to Speak Alzheimer's," by Joanne Koenig Coste[21]), concentrates on things the caregiver can do to meet the patient at whatever place they happen to be. The phrase the author uses more than any other is the advice not to try to reason with a person who has lost the ability to reason!

As I read the book, I discovered a lot of things that we (especially Dad) have done right and quite a few things that we have had to learn from experience. We're pretty close to being on target most of the time. One thing that I gravitated toward was the advice to maintain and support laughter. Even though Maggie has lost a lot of her memories, she does have a quick and ready laugh.

Following the advice of the first book I read, I now try to call Maggie every day on my way home from work. I think she enjoys these short conversations. I've learned what to talk about. One day she got up from the dinner table to come to the phone, so I asked what she was having for dinner, but she didn't remember. Avoiding those sorts of questions, I'm nearly always able to direct things in such a way that we start laughing together.

Cameron, Alastair and Sheila McGown at Kirksville in 1939

I've always enjoyed Maggie's robust belly laughs. When Jamie was here, I told her that my best memories of our trip to Australia happened early in the morning at their place near Melbourne. I remember getting up early for breakfast to find Maggie and her brothers, Cameron and

Alistair, sitting in Alistair's breakfast nook. They were telling stories and laughing uproariously.

The author of a book I'm reading, unrelated to Alzheimer's disease, told a story about how she was reprimanded as a child for laughing too much with her cousin. It's hard to understand how you can get too much of a good thing, but it reminded me of an episode from my childhood. We took a lot of car trips together as a family, and we had to find ways to keep ourselves entertained. Ever since I can remember, we had a station wagon. Jody and I sat in the second seats, Sheila and Lisa were in the back, and Deirdre, our Kerry blue terrier, took turns in the middle and back seats, depending on where she got the most attention.

Often Maggie kept us busy by leading us in songs, such as "She'll Be Coming 'Round the Mountain" and "Oh! Susanna." Failing that, we often played a game in which the object was to tell a story that would make the other person laugh. I think it was Sheila's innovation that the story had to begin with the words, "On the shores of Gitche Gumee, lay an old digestive biscuit …" Jody was always the last to cave, but it was never long before Lisa and I were shrieking with laughter.

Dad, however, was all business whenever we crossed into Canada on our way to our vacation spot at Rondeau. He would solemnly tell us that Customs was no joke and that everything had to be taken very seriously. Of course, we did our best to calm down, but it was no easy matter. I recall one episode when Jody initiated a conspiracy of silence. Our quietness at the border had an unusual quality, so Maggie looked back to see what we were doing. We were biting our lips and squirming to keep from laughing. And there was our dog, Deirdre, ready to greet the Customs officer, panting, with an expression much like a smile on her face, and wearing Lisa's plastic, bright yellow sunglasses.

— Felix

MARCH 13, 2011

Dear Family,

I think there may be two kinds of titles for a book or article. For the first type, I will confess to an inspiration I picked up here in Grand Cayman, from a tiny book on beachcombing. When an unusually large number of flip-flops were found on the East Coast of Florida, the headline in The Wall Street Journal read: "Lost soles: Will a flip-flop flap escalate into a full thong war?" In the same realm, I would put Rabbi Harold Kushner's "When Bad Things Happen to Good People." In both instances, we are drawn to read the material, either because the title is so clever or because it promises to answer a question we really care about.

The second category includes "All I Ever Needed to Know I Learned in Kindergarten" and "Zen and the Art of Motorcycle Maintenance." Few of us might be tempted to read either of these. Most of us never owned a motorcycle, and I'm willing to admit that the title alone says enough for me. In fact, this category could be "why-ruin-a-perfectly-good-title-by-adding-a-book-to-it?"

In one sense, "Learning to Speak Alzheimer's" by Joanne Koenig Coste belongs in the second camp. I didn't start to read it expecting to find startling insights, but it is filled with lots of gentle hints, helpful day-to-day recommendations that any of us might be able to apply to situations with a person in early or mid-stage Alzheimer's.

According to Coste, because of memory loss, altered perception and a contraction of vocabulary, we need to adopt a perspective that will help us to see the world as viewed by a patient with Alzheimer's disease. The book offers five tenets:

1) Make the physical environment work.
2) Know that communication remains possible.
3) Focus on remaining skills.
4) Live in the patient's world.
5) Enrich the patient's life.

It all seems logical. What is compelling is the author's concept of "habilitation" and her personal and professional experiences that support that idea. Coste was pregnant with her fourth child when her husband developed dementia in his 40s. Perhaps one of the worst of any mother's fear: Two people in diapers at the same time. She then spent the next 30 years as a professional caregiver for people with Alzheimer's disease and as a leader of Alzheimer's support groups.

One of Coste's anecdotes is illustrative. An 89-year-old woman walked out of her room at the care center and said, "I want to see my mother." The conventional caregiver tried to reason with her and pointed out that she couldn't since her mother was dead. The more she tried to get the patient in touch with reality, the more frustrated the patient became, eventually becoming agitated and combative. She required physical restraint, then a sedative injection. The patient then spent the day sitting in a reclining Geri-chair in view of the nurses. This is an example of reality orientation, which was the common approach until recently.

In the habilitative scenario, the 89-year old woman asks, "I want to see my mother." The modern caregiver responds, "Tell me about her." The patient replies, "She's a great cook. I wish I could cook like her." After asking what the mother liked to cook the best, the caregiver says, "Let's get a cup of coffee. You can talk more there." In the coffee room, the patient soon forgets about her original request for her mother and is glad to have the company of the caregiver. This example fulfilled three of the five tenets: communication is possible, live in the patient's world and enrich the patient's life.

These five tenets appear to be good starting points for any of us, either as family members of or as caregivers to a patient with Alzheimer's. The full value that underlies these may arise from the most important phrase in the title: "Speak Alzheimer's." Often, when we ask someone if they speak a foreign language, we get all sorts of qualifiers: I can understand it better than I speak it; I can read it but not write it. (Or, my favorite, Arnold Klein on French: "Yes, but not well enough to be witty.") We appreciate the complete mastery that we see from an expert interpreter. I think that's what we are called to be for the person with Alzheimer's: someone who can interpret them when their emotions, motives or thoughts are otherwise hidden by memory loss, altered perception and lack of vocabulary.

— Felix

MARCH 17, 2011

Dear Family,

I didn't think of it as a Saint Patrick's Day dinner at first.

I went to my parents' house for dinner tonight. Caroline is at her folks' house, and since we've been in Grand Cayman she was not able to visit.

There are a few predicable things about dinner. One is that the menu will include salmon and sweet potatoes. The intrigue centers on the possibility that the salmon won't be overcooked. Tonight, I called from 10 minutes away. The salmon looked perfect in the frying pan when I arrived.

Maggie was wearing a plaid green dress that buttoned down the front. She was pacing a bit, waiting for at least one more person to arrive for dinner. This has now become a pattern, to anticipate others joining us for dinner.

I recalled the advice from the book I mentioned in my last post. How can I interpret Maggie's repetitive pattern? What is she hoping for? Whatever it was, neither Dad nor I could think of a way to get her to serve the salmon. I suggested as many names as I could think of, people who could not come tonight, so it would be OK to eat. I confess that I looked at the clock and at the salmon, and back again ... 15 minutes passed with us standing quietly in the kitchen. The salmon cooked on.

As soon as Maggie seemed ready to serve, Dad put on his apron and suggested that Maggie do the same. This is just as it is recommended in the book on the language of Alzheimer's. If a person tends to get food on their clothes at dinner, have them wear a pretty apron, and certainly not a child's bib. The caregiver should put on his apron first.

Dad asked about saying grace, and I asked Maggie if she knew a grace for St. Patrick's Day. She didn't, but then she said this:

> *"This is what I know,*
> *It's important that we have St Patrick.*
> *The world needs St. Patrick,*
> *And we need St. Patrick.*
> *It comes back to this,*
> *And so I'm glad we have St. Patrick.*
> *Amen."*

Now, compare that to a segment from the Prayer of St. Patrick:

> *"May Christ be with us!*
> *May Christ be before us!*
> *May Christ be in us,*
> *Christ be over all!*
> *May Thy Salvation, Lord,*
> *Always be ours,*
> *This day, O Lord, and evermore. Amen."*

We had a slow-paced and leisurely dinner. Maggie did most of the talking, rambling on about Vancouver Island. Neither Dad nor I could follow it, but it was clearly pleasant for her. It was a warm, spring-like 64 degrees, and the river was calm under the pale blue sky. Two Canada geese, obviously a couple, held their ground in front of the house at the water's edge. Periodically, the one on the left honked its hoarse call, and I couldn't tell if it was scolding or claiming territory. They bustled about and seemed content.

The salmon was well done, and the sweet potatoes were perfect, as usual.

— Felix

APRIL 21, 2011

Dear Family,

There's a bittersweet aspect to this letter. First, I apologize that I have not written in a month. I have my sights set on a few areas to explore with The Maggie Letters, including cognitive reserve and new information about the genetic aspects of Alzheimer's disease. Both of these topics have implications for all of us in the extended family, given Maggie's and her mother's history. But, these topics also will involve a lot of reading for me, and then the challenge of rendering them into plain, non-medical English. I savor this latter challenge, but I'm short on time now. I wish these letters were my first priority and not something for my discretionary time.

I stopped for dinner with the folks tonight. For once I was on time, about 30-45 minutes earlier than I usually get there. Dinner was ready. We had salmon, potatoes and sauerkraut. I asked about green vegetables. Dad apparently has figured out a way to minimize Maggie's difficulty in getting up to go to the bathroom at night. The schedule is to have fruit in the morning, vegetables at lunch, and potatoes and salmon at dinner. It seems that the water content of the food figures into this plan.

Jody had warned me that it had become more difficult to be with the parents. Maggie has increasing difficulty in keeping up with the conversation, and Dad is hearing less than ever. For example, when I arrived, Dad said, "Are you ready for dinner?" Maggie answered, "No, let's sit and talk awhile." Dad responded, "Good, dinner's ready to go." And he left for the kitchen. Maggie and I followed.

Dad missed several things at dinner, including the news that I had spent time with one of his favorite colleagues from his practice in Detroit. I feel bad that I didn't shout it out a second or third time. As I drove home, I wondered if I might have been guilty of some passive-aggressive behavior, letting my impatience with his refusal to wear hearing aids affect our conversation.

Either way, it was a very quiet time, with Dad not hearing and Maggie not following. We did have this interesting exchange:

Me: "Do you think Sheila will be staying for four or five days when she comes next week?"

Maggie, "Yes, and I expect her to perform just as well as we anticipate."

Then Maggie said she has been so busy that she hasn't seen her brothers at all. Having learned to "speak Alzheimer's," I didn't offer her a reality check but instead changed the subject to Jamie's visit here in January. Maggie was so pleased to learn about the visit.

It was a beautiful, sunny evening. Despite the apparently calm wind, the water was choppy. A couple of double-crested cormorants flew low over the water not far from shore; a large flock of Canada geese arced across the sky to the east. As dinner was ending, a bald eagle flew close to the house. As I called the parents' attention to it, it careened off toward Canada. I don't think Maggie ever saw it because of her macular degeneration. I don't know if Dad heard me. Bald eagles are increasingly common, but it's still a thrill to see one.

The situation is well in control, and Maggie is well-cared for. No rest home could possibly be as lovely as the setting they enjoy. I do regret their increasing isolation. It seems to be inevitable that it will increase. Dad is doing a remarkable job with Maggie. To find an alternative to the situation seems daunting.

— Felix

APRIL 29, 2011

Dear Family,

When Caroline and I stopped at a flower shop on Easter Sunday afternoon, the big sign in the window told us that there was no end to the opportunity to buy flowers: Wednesday was Professional Assistant's Day, formerly "Secretary's Day." Caroline asked what we usually did in our office. The answer was that we usually forgot until 5 p.m. the night before, and then asked some innocent person, anyone who was not a secretary, to try to think of something that we could purchase by 8 a.m. the next day. It was rarely a success. (This year we forgot altogether!)

Caroline then reminded me how Maggie treated the office staff on Secretary's Day. While they all might have been waiting for the chance to be taken out to a restaurant for lunch, Maggie saw this as a chance for a really special treat. She would load up the wicker picnic basket, usually used for the Lenten Potluck Dinners, and take lunch in to the hapless office staff. On the top of the basket, ROGERS was painted in caps with her signature red nail polish. Sturdy paper plates and festive napkins would be passed out. Dad would put on a pot of water for tea. Lunch was likely sandwiches that included aged cheddar cheese from Canada, served on bread that Maggie had made for the occasion.

I think the fact that Maggie had thought of this some days in advance won over the secretarial staff, which under any other circumstance might have preferred lunch out. There may be a life lesson here: a thoughtful and considerate act will win out over "store bought" every time.

I asked the folks about this at dinner tonight. Dad had his well-crafted reasons that he always preferred to eat in, mostly focused on the preparation of the food, and the danger of getting other people's leftovers, even in a fine restaurant.

Maggie didn't recall the episodes at the office, of course, but we did have this interesting exchange. I said that I would need to call Caroline when I got home, to see if she had been able to tape the royal wedding of Prince William and Kate Middleton, since she was at her parents' house in Washington, D.C.

Maggie: "Is there any good reason she just didn't go to the wedding?"

Me: "She didn't get invited."

Maggie: "She didn't? Tell me again, who was getting married?"

I tried to explain that it was William, son of Princess Diana and Prince Charles. That didn't work. I reminded her that Elizabeth was Queen of England, and this was her grandson, marrying a charming woman named Kate. This was all too confusing. So, she asked,

"What brought all of you to England in the first place? How long will you be staying?"

I told her that I would love to go to England, and maybe we could visit Scotland when we were there.

She smiled and seemed to be happy with that answer.

— Felix

MAY 7, 2011

Dear Family,

   The week that includes Mother's Day is usually the most beautiful time here in Michigan. The daffodils are still hanging on, and the tulips are at their best, but it's our flowering trees that make the biggest impression. This year, with our late spring, the Allegheny serviceberry, (Amelanchier laevis) still holds its elegant white flowers that seem to float just off the branches as the flowering crabapples, azaleas and magnolias take center stage.

   It's rained much more than it's been sunny for the last month. Today was no exception. There was a light drizzle as I left for the airport. The grass was a rich, fresh green, and the tree trunks were soaked black from a steady night of rain. The sun wouldn't be up for another half-hour as I set out.

   Halfway to the airport, I drove up behind an old pickup. Large patches of rust covered sections of the truck sides, and squares of brown paint formed blotches over much of a formerly white truck. I thought about those old hulks that sit in little-used harbors, ancient metal ships that would belch diesel smoke if they were to start up, and tremble as they moved out, from a drive shaft warped from years of service.

   At dinner last week, a freighter with the same type of paint job moved slowly down the Detroit River. I remembered how Maggie could look at a barn just ready to collapse and remark, "All it needed was a fresh coat of paint to be just like new." I reminded her of that as we watched the boat go by, but it didn't strike a resonant note.

   As I passed the pickup, I saw that the driver was a well-scrubbed kid of 19 or so. There was a low rumble from a faulty exhaust system. Through a large rust hole, I got a good look at the drive shaft, and it seemed pretty straight.

   At the airport, a few places in front of me at check-in was the male counterpart of this truck. He wore a baggy old jacket. Under his baseball cap, his hair was pulled into a short ponytail, and there was a two-week stubble on his face. His jaw was in constant motion, a type of gnathism probably due to a degenerative disease of the ancient brain centers that control movement, the same areas that are deranged in Parkinson's disease. In contrast, the woman next to me at security was an energetic African-American woman who couldn't wait to tell me how much she liked Detroit. It's home, and she's optimistic about our otherwise dispirited city.

I started a conversation with a different woman, who cleared security with me. By coincidence, we had both chosen socks with whimsical designs appropriate for the TSA security folks. We agreed that their absence of any sense of humor was no reason not to use this as a time for a personal statement. Since she was also en route to New York, I knew she would be thrilled to learn that I planned to see the special exhibit on sauropods, the largest dinosaurs ever, at the American Museum of Natural History. Her smile had enough ambiguity that I couldn't tell if she was genuinely interested, or if she showed confidence that she could give me the slip soon enough and hold to her stereotype that one flew to New York to see all manner of kooks that one didn't find in a bland location like Detroit.

The image of old ships remained with me. I recalled our life-changing trip around the world in 1961. When our ship, the Orcades, stopped in Hong Kong for three days, teams of men swarmed the boat to repaint portions of ship in the humid mid-summer heat. After years of annual painting, the paint was caked on so thickly that paint remover was out of the question. Each man was armed with a ball-peen hammer, which he used to whack away at the ship for his eight-hour day. Each morning we had to leave the ship because of the noise and dust; when we returned for dinner, there was a carpet of paint chips everywhere. And on the third day, they repainted.

After the plane landed, and I was in the cab, I noticed New York City is about a week ahead of Detroit. The leaves on the gingko trees are full-size, and the sycamore leaves nearly so.

And, now that I have arrived, it's time to return to where I started: The impetus for this letter is Mother's Day, and I intended to refer to the time I heard the Dalai Lama in 1993 and his comments on how one honors a person. He was at the University of Michigan to receive the Raoul Wallenberg Award. I was attending with Caroline, our daughter Alison (who was 12 at the time) and our minister from my youth, the Rev. Bob Shank. Alison remarked that His Holiness was so engaging and so comfortable she pictured him meeting us down at breakfast. I suspect the flowing saffron robe contributed to this impression. He commented that the way to honor a person was not to recite the list of accomplishments, but rather to emulate their values and actions.

On the occasion of Mother's Day, that's a daunting task! To this point, the letter has been one long tangent, and Maggie loved tangents, so I'm on

solid ground there. But how else do I honor her? I hope that these Maggie
Letters by themselves, as an antemortem eulogy are one way to honor her.
Maggie's annual Christmas Letter was awaited by so many of her friends
and family. At first, she used onionskin typing paper and as many pieces
of carbon paper as could be jammed into her Smith Corona typewriter.
The invention of the Xerox copier solved that problem and allowed more
copies. You have to wonder what she would have done with email. She
had such an artistic flair, she might have been a blogger! She always
allowed herself until Easter to get the Christmas Letter in the mail.

   — Felix

MAY 9, 2011

Dear Family,

   This letter returns to the scientific aspects of Alzheimer's disease. I
know that this approach may put some of you immediately to sleep, but I
ask you to bear with me, and make it at least to the end of this paragraph
before you hit the delete key. I want to address the topic of cognitive
reserve, and its implications in terms of whether you or I might develop
Alzheimer's disease. About 5 percent of Alzheimer's disease is definitely
related to genetic features, but the rest, or 95 percent of cases, are
sporadic, unrelated to inherited factors. Since Maggie and her mother
both had Alzheimer's disease, it seems likely to me that all of us with
McGown lineage are at greater risk to develop it.

   One approach to the question of our likelihood to develop
Alzheimer's disease would be to measure something that differed
between people who had it and those who didn't. Since the accumulation
of the beta-amyloid protein in the brain is a key feature of the disease,
it could be measured in a blood test or in a sample of spinal fluid, or it
might be visualized in a brain imaging test, like a CT scan or an MRI
scan with special biologic markers so the amyloid particles light up. A
new disease classification of Alzheimer's has been promoted recently, in
part based on these new markers. Another approach would be to perform
quantitative measurements of memory and psychological function to
determine neurological status. The results of such studies are reported
with considerable frequency in both lay and scientific literature.

   All of the tests have one common characteristic: Each is good
for about 80 percent of the population they test. The remainder of

subjects just doesn't fit the model. For example, tests of serum levels of beta-amyloid, the putative agent in Alzheimer's disease, show a clear relationship between test levels and the incidence of the disease; that is, the higher the level, the greater the disease incidence in most patients. However, there are substantial numbers of patients with high blood serum levels and no clinical evidence of Alzheimer's disease. This parallels the findings from autopsy and brain imaging studies, where a significant number of subjects show significant disease burden but no clinical evidence of dementia.

For about 20 years now, scientists have struggled to explain this discrepancy. The best way to understand this, it appears, is that certain people have greater resistance to succumbing to the disease process than others. That is, there must be a difference in reserve function that allows certain of us to tolerate higher levels of loss of nerve cells before dementia becomes manifest. There are two major theories that may explain this, and a combination of the two mechanisms is a likely consideration.

Brain reserve is one major idea. In this view, the ability of a person to withstand the alterations of Alzheimer's disease (or a stroke, for that matter) depends on the total number of neurons that a person has at the onset of the disease. In support of this theory is the correlation between brain size (and even head circumference) and resistance to cognitive decline with Alzheimer's disease or stroke. The idea is that there is a certain threshold, an absolute number of neurons that a person must have in order to be neurologically intact.

Two patients each have the same degree of brain injury, but only one develops dementia, because she didn't start with as many neurons, and the injury caused her to fall below the threshold value. The brain reserve model is one in which the reserve is passive; it depends only on the total number brain cells or synaptic connections the person has. This model is analogous to the "hardware" of a computer.

In contrast, the theory of cognitive reserve states that a person who does not develop Alzheimer's uses networks more efficiently, or utilizes parallel pathways less subject to disruption by the disease process. There may be an additional aspect of compensation, where the person uses structures or neural networks that are not normally available in order to compensate for the nerve damage. This model is analogous to the "software" by which a computer operates.

It makes sense that both mechanisms will be at play in some individuals. For convenience, the term "cognitive reserve" has come to include both brain reserve and cognitive reserve as described above.

If you're still with me, the logical question has to be, "Is there anything that I can do to enhance my cognitive reserve and ward off Alzheimer's disease?" Several factors have been associated with cognitive reserve, and these may provide relative protection against Alzheimer's.[26] These include:

Education

The level of education attained correlates with the risk of clinical expression of Alzheimer's disease but not of neuropathological findings. Education doesn't protect against amyloid deposition, but it does modify the clinical evidence of Alzheimer's. There is better cognitive function for each year of additional education.

Occupation

Higher lifetime occupational attainment decreases the risk for dementia.

Physical activities

In the animal model, exercise stimulates the growth of new nerve cells. In humans, it increases cerebral blood flow, cerebral nutrient supply and enhances the sensitivity of cortical receptors. Exercise also seems to stimulate trophic factors and neuronal growth, even at adult and advanced age. These effects seem to be causal, and exercise is not just a marker of good health.

Social and intellectual activities

This invokes the phrase "use it, or lose it." The activities that are protective are remarkably diverse. They include traveling, doing odd jobs, knitting, community activities, gardening and maintaining an extensive social network. Beneficial leisure activities include reading magazines, playing cards or bingo, going to classes, playing musical instruments and dancing.

The idea of cognitive reserve as a compensation is based on a newer understanding of neuroplasticity. When I was in medical school, we were taught that we are born with a certain number of brain cells, and there is no way to increase them or to change their function. We now know that learning and a physically and socially enriched environment may increase synaptic density (the total number of nerve connections), which may make for more efficient cognitive function in the unaffected neurons.

Environmental factors may be at play as well. Environmental factors may both decrease neuro-degeneration and enhance brain repair and recovery. Conversely, differential exposure to neurotoxins (such as pollution), heavy drinking, malnutrition, higher rates of cerebrovascular disease, and poorer quality healthcare and access may account for higher rates of Alzheimer's disease.

The overlap of these areas is considerable. People with low educational level are likely to have lower occupational achievement and in turn be at increased risk for exposure to some of these negative effects.

Here's my bottom line: I think it's likely that all of us with McGown lineage are at an increased risk to develop Alzheimer's disease. It might be useful to pursue an idea I brought up a few months ago, that is, to look into our family tree. When I suggested it before, the intent was to bring our Australian and American cousins together. Now an additional goal would be to see if there are other incident cases of dementia in Maggie's cousins or other relatives.

I'm encouraged that Maggie didn't manifest Alzheimer's until her late 80s, even though her mother had serious cognitive decline in her early 70s. I think Maggie attenuated her risk by her level of education, her overall good health and her many leisure activities. I think it is premature for any of us to consider undergoing any tests for Alzheimer's, whether blood tests, spinal fluid analysis or a brain imaging study. If the tests were to be positive, presently there is no effective medicine. Instead, we would just have a greater incentive to pursue a healthier lifestyle in order to enhance our cognitive reserve. Isn't it logical to do that now, even without any testing?

— Felix

CHAPTER FIVE

Progressive Decline Calls for 24-Hour Care

MAY 27, 2011

Dear Family,

When I saw the folks last weekend, Dad looked old and tired. Since he turns 91 in August, the old should be no surprise. It's the tired part that was of concern.

I had gone to their house to put flowers in the garden by the driveway for Maggie. Years ago, I ran out of fresh ideas for something to buy her for Mother's Day (or Christmas or her birthday, for that matter). About 10 years ago, I came up with the idea of a garden that I would put in around Mother's Day. It's been a good tradition, modified each year by my ongoing experience with the increasing local deer population. As their numbers grow, their diet becomes increasingly nonselective, and they now eat most of the things found on the list of plants that are considered to be deer-proof.

When I got to the house, I found the folks in the living room. They were sitting quietly next to each other with no TV, no radio, no music. Dad was in one of the now-dilapidated large easy chairs that were in the living room at Sunset Lodge in the early 1960s, and Maggie was in a straight back chair next to it, facing in the same direction. Dad always encourages her to sit in a chair like that, since it's easier to help her up. We agreed that I would do my work first and then come back for tea.

Planting the garden just took an hour. When I returned, they were seated in the same positions, but Dad, meantime, had been up to get tea ready. The water was simmering, and he had organic blueberry pancakes to go with it. I had brought some gluten-free chocolate-covered cookies for Maggie. Since Dad has determined that sugar contributes to brain degeneration, I had to come up with a sugar content that would be acceptable. I think my number was a good compromise between the truth and the level he would be comfortable with.

Over tea, Dad talked about his current problem. He wasn't asking for advice, since that's not his way, but he did lay the issue out in such manner that it was clear he didn't have a solution. There are two problems. Maggie seems to have progressive difficulties with nocturnal urinary incontinence. Dad's solution is to waken her every three hours for a pre-emptive trip to the potty. I think that led to the second issue, which is that Dad has sprained his back and now has pain in both legs as well. Lisa thinks it might be polymyalgia rheumatica, a painful condition of the elderly, which fortunately, is self-terminating after a few weeks or months.

I asked about alternatives. Could Maggie wear a disposable diaper? Did the Alzheimer's Association have any advice? Dad doesn't want Maggie to lie in a wet diaper, so he considers that off the table. And he's says he's read everything there is to read on the topic, so that any possible alternatives, should they exist, seem closed to discussion as well. He hoped that some family members, namely some great-grandkids, might be willing to sleep on the couch in the living room and get Maggie up every three hours. Part of the problem is that Maggie is so hard to awaken at night. I told Dad that people in their 20s don't awaken very well at night either!

He didn't warm to my suggestion that it might be appropriate to bring someone in for the night shift. Eighteen months ago, Dad and I squared off over the issue of help in the home. Our recommendation was 24-hour care, and the compromise was to have Stephanie come in for a day shift five times a week. I suggested a name of another caregiver. After talking a bit more, Dad agreed to ask Stephanie if she had any friend(s) who might be interested.

We are at a turning point. The reality is that Dad can't handle things anymore by himself. He's been remarkable up to now, continuing to work in the office as he also has done the shopping, cooking and dinner cleanup. Progressive fatigue is taking its toll, now made worse by his back and leg pain. I know he resists giving up control. I think he has always assumed that with planning, good skills and determination, he could do whatever was needed.

When we were young, Dad liked to tell the story of John Henry, the strongest man on the railroad crew. When the steam-driven pile driver was invented, the question came up: Could it outperform a man and then replace him on the crew? John Henry faced off against the machine and matched it, driving railroad ties, one by one. Problem was, he died at the end of his Herculean day.

We have two areas of sadness here. Dad is now forced to face new realities in his care for Maggie. And Maggie has made one more step in her relentless downhill path. The most telling sign was that Dad led this entire discussion sitting next to Maggie as if she didn't comprehend any of it. I'm sad to note that he was right.

— Felix

MAY 28, 2011

Dear Family,

I'm in northern Ontario at the moment, and Caroline is in the Washington, D.C., area visiting her parents. We spoke by telephone last night. She is concerned that her father is becoming more forgetful, and that, because of this, her mother is increasingly tired and stressed. As we spoke, a feeling crept into the conversation that we need to steel ourselves for the inevitable need to attend to them as well.

When Jody, Sheila, Lisa and I were in high school, Dad ran a discussion group in our home. The focus of the group was "The Fourth Way," a compilation of the talks of P.D. Ouspensky, a Russian mathematician and philosopher who died in 1947. I often did my homework in the room next to the meeting — and also did my share of eavesdropping.

I've returned often to an image that Ouspensky described in another of his books. As he was walking in St. Petersburg before World War I, he saw a truck loaded with crutches. His concern was that they were crutches for a war that had not yet started and for legs that had not yet been injured or blown off.

For years, this vision came to my mind, and I couldn't understand why it had such an impact on him. Only lately has it occurred to me that that it symbolizes something that's happened too often in my own life. I now realize how much time I spend with imaginary battles that haven't actually occurred. I've rehearsed my part over and over for conflicts that likely will never happen.

As I remembered it, Ouspensky had two important recommendations. One is that we try to remember ourselves (i.e., "I am here"), and the second is that we practice stopping thoughts. In line with a Maggie Letter that I posted several months ago, these ideas correlate with aspects we know concerning how the brain functions. The default brain is the place our thoughts go when we aren't thinking about anything, and it consists largely of daydreams and imagination. This part of the brain is closely aligned with the narrative self, so our personal lives get caught up in these thoughts. It's common for negative emotions to creep in. Anxiety and depression live here. Remembering ourselves and stopping thoughts involves keeping guard over our attention monitoring.

Here in Canada, I have lots more time than usual for contemplative reading. At the moment, a common thread in my reading touches on what happens to us when we stop the thoughts of the narrative self and allow our "true self" to be on its own, protected from the incessant whirl of daydreams. The readings include Quaker ideas, Buddhism, the Kabbalah and modern psychology. The vocabulary differs, but the idea is basically the same: When we stop thoughts, our mind naturally moves to heal itself. The outcome is a more peaceful, serene outlook. A natural accompaniment is more loving behavior.

Since I'm at a stage when I spend a good deal of time looking back, I see lots of wasted time when I let imaginary battles sap my time and energy. As Caroline and I are learning, our inevitable task is to take care of our family in the most loving way. This seems to be the most important part of the life journey.

We are both so excited that our daughter Beth is expecting a baby boy in August. We also realize that we need to look forward to a grandchild and a parent in diapers at the same time.

— Felix

JUNE 11, 2011

Dear Family,

The first thing I did when I got to my parents' house Wednesday was to stop at the garden I had put in for Maggie as her annual Mother's Day gift. It looked good: the foxglove has bloomed on two-foot stems, and the Maltese cross was getting started with its fire-engine red flowers. The deer didn't appear to have eaten anything. Jody had sprayed the plants with a concoction made of unmentionable bodily fluids of animals we wish we had never heard of, and it apparently worked.

When I got to the door, the air was rich with the fragrance of the large white peonies in front of the house. Inside, Maggie and Dad were in the same seats as described in my previous notes. Dad was in shorts and Maggie in a long skirt and billowy blouse. She was reading a card.

Since the folks no longer have an evening meal, Dad had a bowl of chips for me as a snack. Smaller than a cereal bowl, it was bigger than a sake cup, so I had no complaints. We sat and talked, trying to catch up, as it had been a couple weeks since my last visit. As we talked, Maggie didn't seem engaged. She just read and re-read the same card and then handed it to me without speaking. It was the Mother's Day card I had given her in May. The plants on the cover had filigree leaves and curlicue stems. In the lower right corner, a bright pink lady bug was watering with a portable can that seemed to make stardust water droplets. It occurred to me that we all ought to send Maggie some cards periodically.

I talked with Dad about the memories I had of peonies as a kid on Grosse Ile. Our neighbors to the north, the Overholts, had large peony beds. We were fascinated by the hordes of ants that covered the tight flower buds just before they opened. Dad said that they served a purpose for the flower, but I've since learned that's a suburban legend.

When we crossed into the Overholt's yard, we loved to do so by jumping over the peony beds. As barefoot kids, we often didn't clear them in a single bound, and our feet would knock the blooms off and send the petals flying. Dad said his recollection was that you always knew when a big rain was coming, because the peonies were at their peak. That is, until they got soaked by the rain and sagged over onto the ground.

As we spoke, an osprey cruised down the river. I interrupted the talk and pointed vigorously, "Look at that bird!"

Dad glanced up and calmly answered, "Yes, those are the sailboat races."

"No," I said, "I'm talking about that huge bird."

"The sailboats race every Wednesday on the Canadian side," he responded.

Finally, I jumped up and gestured so hysterically that both of them finally looked. Just then, the osprey careened in our direction. It headed straight for the house, right where we were sitting. As it got very close, it banked to its left, showing its trademark black eye stripe, and then returned to the river, heading south. Osprey is one of my favorite birds. With a wingspan up to 6 feet, they are formidable raptors.

Maggie resumed looking at her card. Then she began to read it out loud, over and over. Each time was different, and the choice of words was uniquely hers. Each reading, however, ended the same way, "Have a great day. Love, Felix."

— Felix

JUNE 19, 2011

Dear Family,

The Father's Day celebration was a big success. Jody and Rosemary had their yard and house looking fantastic. I was especially impressed with the gardens, where the plantings looked great, and all of the weeds were pulled. Caroline said it was because Jody had conscripted Rosemary, Lindsey and Rachel to get all the work done.

Looking back, we had the best turnout of family members at any event in recent past, except a wedding, which gets all of us there. Sheila was in from Oklahoma, Lisa from Cleveland, and I came straight from work. We had lots of family members, too. Besides Caroline, our daughter Elizabeth was there with 7/9th of a child, but looking as if she could deliver at any day. Sheila's daughters, Mona and Rose, were there and Sheila's husband, Frank, had his son and daughter, and their friends. Lisa had Lord Bentley, of course.

Jody and Rosemary had toyed with the idea of all of us bringing food, since there are so many individual preferences: organic, vegan, gluten-free, raw, fat-free, fat-rich, sugar-free and I-really-don't-care foods. Amazingly, they got everything at Whole Foods, and we served ourselves in buffet style. Champagne helped ease any rough spots that may have been present.

Maggie was in good spirits, and seemed much more engaged than when I had seen her last. She sat with Dad, who was very attentive to her. She seemed to enjoy the cards and presents. Dad was very pleased with all of the attention, which is not usually his style.

— Felix

JULY 30, 2011

Dear Family,

Today had been mapped out to be the day I could complete the arduous yard work that's been hanging over my head and also finish off a medical manuscript with which I've struggled for four months. Instead, I went to a funeral, visited Maggie and weeded her garden, and then went to my first movie in a year.

The funeral was touching. My high school classmate Terry died last week, after a long battle with a progressive lung disease that was only diagnosed fully in the last few months. He was a scratch golfer, which I learned means he was good. What it means for a funeral is that it's 50 percent golf stories and 50 percent Roman Catholic liturgy. His eldest son gave one of the eulogies. He said his father was never heard to speak ill of anyone, but he did guess that he might have done so in rare circumstances. It reminded me of the person who so values their children that they don't use foul language in front of them. And what is more foul than speaking ill of someone else?

I called after the funeral to tell Dad that I would go to the wake and get to his house for lunch in about an hour. He told me lunch was all prepared, but it would be fine to get there at 12:30 p.m. When I got there, Maggie and Dad were sitting at the table, and lunch was ready. Dad had put out the basics for make-your-own tacos. He served Maggie first, then himself, and then I made mine. He asked Maggie to say grace. This is what she said:

> *"Dear Lord, we give you thanks for so much. So many things have happened to us. I don't know why, but they did. Amen."*

Dad noted that Maggie's prayers are always on the mark. Lunch was pleasant. Large sailboats churned through the Detroit River in a race from Belle Isle to Lake Erie. We're in the midst of a hot spell here in Detroit, and the air was still in the house with just a hint of air movement. Dad says they have some air conditioning, but it seems to be subtle and understated.

At lunch, I told Dad about a classmate I saw at the wake, a lawyer he knows well. His mother had fallen earlier during the week while she was home alone. She activated the card on a necklace she wore, and the fire department arrived minutes later and took her to the hospital. I suggested that Dad might get something like this. He said it was an interesting idea and changed the subject to the lawyer's daily drive time to work.

I may just buy a medical alert bracelet for his birthday, which comes up in a few weeks. We do have a tradition of buying something that we think the household should have, more than the recipient might want it.

The movie was "Midnight in Paris" by Woody Allen. I love Paris, and the photography was beautiful. The movie was all about nostalgia and the longing to live in a better time, sometime in the past that we have romanticized.

It was a day to savor some of the great ontological questions, like: What is life? And, am I living it to the fullest? Each day we have that gift, but today juxtaposed them in sharp relief.

— Felix

AUGUST 13, 2011

Dear Family,

I may have had a taste of what an Alzheimer's patient could experience. This morning I drove to work listening to classical radio. In the midst of the usual music, they played a piece that felt like a country hoe-down.

The song reminded me of an event from the early 1970s, but I could only recall fragments of what happened. One summer evening, I was driving south through Iowa. I pulled off the road and went to a music festival. When I arrived, they were doing square dance calls. I danced with a pretty woman, who told me her name, but I didn't ask for her phone number or where she lived. I remember the sky was a clear twilight blue, with no clouds and low humidity. This may have been where I first learned the dance, "Dive for the oyster, dip for the clam."

Here's what I don't know: I must have been with someone that night; it's just too uncharacteristic of me to get off the road for any reason. (I drive the car until the fuel gauge is just a little below empty. I never like to make an unnecessary stop.) Who could have been with me? And where had we been? How could I have been in Iowa when I was enrolled at Kirksville, Missouri? If my passenger was a woman named Lois (my best guess because she was so spontaneous about things), what happened next? What about the music and my drive today triggered this memory of an event that happened nearly 40 years ago?

In the car today, I tried hard to put the rest of the story together. It was frustrating to deal with a few vivid fragments but not be able to pull things into a cohesive whole. There is no one in my current set of friends and family who can help me. I could imagine turning this over and over in my head in an effort to complete the story or at least to make sense. I thought of the people I've seen with Alzheimer's who keep repeating the same story fragment over and over. Maggie did that over a year ago when she kept recalling a boat ride that Jody took her on.

The radio host told me that the piece was "Appalachian Barn Dance," by Apollo's Fire Baroque Ensemble. Just in case any of you are on tenterhooks about the square dance, I went looking for my journals that I kept when I was in medical school, and I was pleased to find the journal entry. It was instructive to see how I had remembered things incorrectly. On September 23, 1972, "several of us went to the Country & Western and Bluegrass Festival in Drakesville, Iowa." I didn't have a moment of spontaneity after all! The pretty woman was Peggy, and my short entry described her as very beautiful, "openly friendly and not afraid of physicality." She was 19 and engaged to a guy named Joe from Syracuse. On the topic of marriage, my journal had this enigmatic entry, quoting her as saying, "It's unfortunate that city life insists that things be done outside the family, for instance, rock and roll versus square dancing."

I wasn't anxious about the gaps in my memory because I knew I could go to the radio playlist and to my journal, but I wonder how a patient with Alzheimer's disease might feel?

Permit me two sidebars from the world of neurophysiology. First, on the tendency to remember a pretty woman so vividly, neuroscientist David Eagleman says this has roots in evolutionary biology. Part of our hardwiring as men is to be constantly on the lookout for the best opportunity to enhance our gene pool.[27] I'm reminded that while it's still not socially acceptable to be gazing across the room, there are reasons for it.

Second, a good deal of my memory was faulty. How is it that we remember things that didn't happen? This is a new field in research. Certain people do it more than others, including victims of sexual abuse and, of course, victims of alien abduction.[28] It has implications for interviewing patients, witnesses and individuals of interest to historians. Isn't the brain a remarkable thing?

It's possible this event was triggered because I'm looking forward and looking back: I now have had 10 days of experience as a grandfather. Beth gave birth to Theodore Hays Hamilton on August 3, 2011. Fortunately, "grandfather" is largely an honorary position.

— Felix

AUGUST 26, 2011

Dear Family

I'm up in northern Ontario again. With the much-anticipated birth of our first grandchild, Caroline did not want to plan any vacation time, in order to be available to help Beth during those first few weeks of intense sleep deprivation. I carved out a few days, just in case she changed her mind. Caroline decided instead to visit her parents in the Washington, D.C., area, since her father has a broken foot and needs extra attention.

As I pulled a few things together to bring with me, I was determined to work on The Maggie Letters since the serenity and solitude here would be enriching. I packed The McGown Papers, and I hope to write about them soon. I also brought a book of poetry, which caught my eye as I was getting things together.

Sometime in the last two years, I arrived at work to find a book on the center of my desk. There was no note with the book and no inscription inside. Instead, the corner of page 82 was turned over. The book is "Twenty Poems to Nourish Your Soul."[29]In the middle of page 82 are five quotes on the virtues of simplicity. I pondered the quotes and wondered who left this. The most likely suspect was sufficiently coy that I really couldn't be sure who gave this to me. The quotes were part of a commentary on a poem by U.S. poet laureate Billy Collins. I didn't relate to the poem, so the book was set aside.

As I turned the book over in my hands before I left on this trip, I looked again at page 82, and my eyes went to the bottom of the page: "… simplifying our life is so complex that many of us feel compelled to sign up for a workshop to break it down into simple steps." I didn't feel the need for a workshop, but I did think this might make interesting reading in the place that already works so well to nourish my soul.

And since I admit that I nourish my soul through a systematic approach to things, I started with page ix, the foreword. It took me 30 minutes to get to the first poem. The book is arranged by themes, and the first two poems focus on attention. "The Summer Day" by Mary Oliver ends with these lines:

"… Tell me, what is it you plan to do / with your one wild and precious life?"

Today I moved on to the second poem, "The Layers" by Stanley Kunitz. It includes these lines:

"… When I look behind,
as I am compelled to look
before I can gather strength
to proceed on my journey,
I see the milestones dwindling
toward the horizon
and the slow fires trailing
from the abandoned campsites,
over which scavenger angels
wheel on heavy wings …"

Basswood Lake has always tugged at my sense of self, because it defines three milestones. The lake itself rests in a granite bowl that is part of the Precambrian Shield, which gives northern Ontario much of its rugged beauty. The Precambrian era spans the time of 545 million to 2.5 billion years ago. I compromise at its midpoint of approximately 1.2 billion years ago, just to have a specific date when I look at the bedrock on which our cottage is built. Then the glaciers scraped all of this rock bare during the Wisconsin Glacial Episode 10,000 to 13,000 years ago. Just moss a few inches thick, patches of wild blueberry and a few rugged pine trees have found their place in the rocks that surround the lake. The third milestone happens today with me looking out at a sparkling blue lake on a crystal clear morning.

Two weeks from now would normally be the time for the annual trip up here with Lisa, Maggie and Dad. We took the trip for 10 years or so, long enough to have a pattern to our travels. We would drive up in two segments, stopping in Petoskey, Michigan, as the halfway point. Once up here, we also had a few patterns. Dad brought in firewood and kept the fire going, even if it wasn't entirely needed for heating the cottage. Maggie helped me dig potatoes from the garden I planted each spring. This year, Dad says they won't try to make the trip. It would present just too many challenges for Maggie.

Our cottage, Windhover, is now "an abandoned campsite" for Maggie, and maybe Dad, for that matter. Speaking of poetry, Windhover is named for the poem of the same name by Gerard Manly Hopkins (1844-1889),[30] which happens to also be the inspiration for this book of poetry I brought with me on this trip.

Early one morning, Hopkins caught sight of the windhover, the name for a falcon known as a common kestrel. And he wrote:

"... *My heart in hiding/Stirred for a bird — the achieve of, the mastery of the thing!*"

Moved by the "Brute beauty and valour and act," he found in the windhover his "chevalier," the "kingdom of daylight's dauphin."

Isn't this a more inspiring image than Stanley Kunitz' scavenger angels that wheel on heavy wings?
   — Felix

August 27, 2011
Dear Family,

I've finally finished reading The McGown Papers. Cousin Jamie Jackson mailed them in late June, but I didn't find them until August, such is the state of my clutter and priorities: I seem to save the mail for the last. Alison was home from New York when I opened the envelope. Alison got started first and was soon so captivated that she stayed up until she finished them in the early hours of the morning. On the other hand, it's taken me two weeks to find the time to read through them. I'm often glad that I don't get placed in a remedial position in life, given my very slow reading, virtual inability to type and clueless status in regard to popular culture.

The McGown Papers consist of several notebooks and other papers collected by Alexander Buchanan McGown. "A.B.," as he was known to his friends and wife, was born in 1830 and died in 1901. He was Maggie's paternal grandfather. In 1987, his letters were transcribed and edited by Maggie's cousin, William G. Young. We knew of him as her Cousin Willie, who was the Presbyterian Bishop of Pakistan and had some renown because he had translated the Bible into Urdu, the native Pakistani tongue.

A. B. McGown
about 1890

Cousin Willie describes my maternal great-grandfather as "quite a character, with a wide variety of interests and a keen sense of humour, especially in his younger days." A.B. McGown started as a pattern designer, but failed to make a living at it, so he tried running a shop. In 1863, he sold his shop and went to Buenos Aires, Argentina, to try his hand at sheep farming. This failed to bring the return he hoped for, so he returned to Scotland in 1869. He got employment in the Paisley Savings Bank in 1873 and worked his way up to actuary, a position he held until his

A. B. McGown in 1859

death. He married Jane Oliver when he was 50 years old. The elder of his two daughters, Maggie Jane, died in 1890 of diphtheria. The other daughter, Janet, was the mother of Willie. There were two sons, Alexander (Maggie's father) and Oliver.

The longest account is the "Diary of the First Voyage" in 1863. The diary may have been written for his mother, and the version Cousin Willie worked from was a typed copy. His account is fascinating, even though it is but a daily record of his time aboard the ship "Joan Taylor" en route to Argentina. Each entry

Jane McGown
nee Oliver

details the time he got up ("turned out") and retired at night ("turned in"). Sometimes there is no more to the entry than that. Other entries give hints of the tedium of the 1863 journey that began February 22 and ended May 4. There are interesting glimpses of life at sea, including his descriptions of storms and of becoming becalmed at the equator on April Fools' Day as well as a few descriptions of his brother William, who joined him on this journey, and of the captain of the ship.

The McGown Papers also include A.B.'s description of his participation in a military ceremony for Queen Victoria and an enthusiastic description of the gaucho of Argentina. His writing has vivid detail, charm and energy. Unfortunately, there is no record of his six years in Argentina, which must have been interesting. He got lodging and apparently received a loan from William Barbour (1828-1891), a friend and brother-in-law to his father, who at the time was living in Argentina, and elsewhere described as "one of Paisley's richest men."

A major section of The Papers involves lists of family members and a family tree assembled by Cousin Willie and his father, the Rev. John Young. It turns out that the McGowns are traced back to Belfast, Ireland. A.B.'s father, John McGown, was born in Ballymacarret, near Belfast, in 1792. His father David was a weaver in Ireland and joined the rebels who were later defeated, forcing him to flee to Glasgow (possibly in 1798). John McGown's obituary describes him as "strictly honest, industrious to a fault, very sober, very active and rigidly upright, and the worst that any person could say of him, that he was an 'Irishman.'"

Besides the family tree, the lists include all manner of other details about the family. My niece Jenn Rogers pointed me to the website Ancestry.com, and I'd love to start filling the McGown family data into a framework and then build on that with new information. Since I'm still in northern Ontario without regular Internet access, let me look at the site and tell you exactly what I'm looking for before you send me any information about your families.

— Felix

P.S. Line drawings from old photographs were made by Miss Claire Mackintosh of Culbokie, Scotland and are part of The McGown Papers.

CHAPTER SIX

Celebrating What Remains

SEPTEMBER 12, 2011

Dear Family,

As I've mentioned before, a basic rule in dealing with people who have Alzheimer's disease is not to mourn the things they have lost but to celebrate the things they still have. For Maggie, her sense of humor, at this point, is still very much intact!

This was borne out Wednesday last week, the day we celebrated my father's 91st birthday. We met at Jody and Rosemary's house. With their daughters, Rachel and Lindsey, they prepared a Mexican feast, including all sorts of organic tacos and burritos, including some that were gluten-free. We gathered on the patio and enjoyed a beautiful summer evening. At the end of the meal, we took a few pictures. The photos make the members of the gathering appear relaxed. The photo shoot didn't start that way. As I tried to move Maggie while seated in her chair, so we would be close together, the chair scraped along on the patio stones. She made a horrible sound and then contorted her face, so she looked very frightened. We all fell for it, so she did it again with even more drama. Only after we were all reassured that she was playing with us could we break into peals of laughter. She got us all!

— Felix

OCTOBER 10, 2011

Dear Family,

On my recent visits with Maggie, I've watched her facial expressions as Dad and I have talked. Dad has had some major back problems, and several visits have just focused on him, rather than trying to bring Maggie into the conversation.

Sometimes she just sits with a dull, blank look, as if she is bored, but often Maggie's eyes follow the conversation. Even at her advanced stage of Alzheimer's disease, I can look at her and not determine the extent of her cognitive decline by her appearance.

One of the tragedies of Alzheimer's disease is that it is typically far advanced at the time of diagnosis. If we had a meaningful treatment for the disease, this would be like making the diagnosis of cancer only when it is widely metastatic. Since there is no effective treatment, it really doesn't matter.

The neurological basis of Alzheimer's has a lot to do with why patients may conceal the diagnosis from us until it is far advanced. To look at this further, I went back and revisited the default brain, one of the fascinating aspects to our lives, which has implications for Alzheimer's patients and for our own quality of life. Alzheimer's disease preferentially attacks the default brain, which among other things, is involved with memory, our sense of self and daydreaming. (Daydreaming may be too harsh a word. The scientific phrase for mind-wandering is "stimulus independent thought," or SIT, meaning that the thoughts arrive spontaneously.)

In 2006, apparently before the term default brain was used, an interesting article appeared in *Science* magazine.[31] It started with the observation that the brain represents only 2 percent of the body mass, but it uses 20 percent of the body's energy. The researchers addressed the question: What fraction of this energy is directly related to brain function? It is estimated that 60-80 percent of the energy budget supports communication among neurons and their supporting cells. The additional energy burden associated with responding to demands of the environment may be as little as 0.5 to 1.0 percent of the total energy budget. (It's daunting to think that only 1 percent or so of our brain activity is used for purposeful activity. In "Defending Your Life," the movie starring Meryl Streep and Albert Brooks, some highly advanced people claimed to use their brain up to 3 or 4 percent of the time. Of course, they were immediately challenged!)

Some findings are intriguing. For example, in the visual cortex, which responds to external input from the retina, less than 10 percent of all synapses carry information from the eye. The rest of the neurons seem to spend their time "talking with each other." (The way I understand this, these other neurons are constantly busy so that an image we see can instantly "make sense" because it fits into a context based on past experience. It may also explain why two people can look at the same thing and see something very different. This default brain is the seat of our individuality, after all.)

Lacking another term for this intrinsic activity of the brain, the authors referred to this as the "dark energy" of the brain, borrowing the term from the field of astronomy. I think this intrinsic activity would be incorporated into the default brain with our current terminology.

In the 19th century, a Bengali mystic[32] described the brain in terms of a mighty tree filled with monkeys, all swinging from branch to branch, chattering incessantly. Anyone who has tried to meditate can surely relate to that analogy. Efforts to focus on a mantra or to maintain mindfulness seem to last just a few seconds or so before the chattering takes over.

In this context, the chattering monkeys are the default brain, and the aspect of our brain that tries to control our thoughts is the executive function. The executive function, the part that we control, is also the part that responds to the environment. For example, when we ask a person a question, the executive brain can give a simple answer. The answer, and the behavior of an Alzheimer's patient in other respects, may be so plausible that we miss an underlying cognitive deficit.

The default brain is much more than a tree filled with chattering monkeys, however. The intrinsic activity of the brain is cohesive and highly organized. This is the part of our brain that takes over for us when we move from learning a task to doing it without thinking. An example is driving a car. When we are learning how to do it, we exert all our powers of concentration on the task. Later, we are able talk on the phone as we drive because our executive function has turned the process of driving the car over to the default brain. (I bet some of us also daydream about some other topic as we talk on the phone while we drive in the car, like what we will have for dinner. In other words, our daydreaming function can address two topics at once, multi-tasking, if you will.)

While the default brain gets us through most of our daily activities, and is therefore essential to us, it's not always our friend. Due to daydreaming, we've all experienced how we can miss out on important parts of our day as we get distracted. Further, because daydreaming is connected to memory and sense of self, we can also find ourselves in imaginary conversations. The default brain is also the seat of depression and other forms of mental illness. Although we invoke executive function to control the default brain, the intrinsic default brain activity causes it to intrude on our lives constantly.

The Alzheimer's patient loses default brain function first, while the executive function remains intact. Huge chunks of brain real estate may disappear before outsiders notice anything. We become aware of gaps in memory first, but other aspects of losing default function only become clear with more advanced stages of the disease.

So, here's the irony: Those of us with intact cognitive function find ourselves mostly under the control of the default brain, and those with Alzheimer's maintain executive function, but there is nothing for it to control.

— Felix

OCTOBER 31, 2011

Dear Family,

Balderdash!

I don't think I've ever heard anyone else use this word except Maggie. It's not unique to her, since I found it in the Oxford English Dictionary. It dates from 1596 and may have its roots in the word "froth." Froth, at that time, referred to a mixture of liquors, such as beer and milk or beer and wine. It came to be a senseless jumble of words, or trash.

I remember it ringing in my ears when I was about 10, and I had asked Maggie if we could buy our costumes for Halloween. No, she said, we'll put our costumes together with things from around the house, just as we always do. It was also the pattern of both of our neighboring families, the Overholts and the Deerings, to make everything from scratch.

I'm so persistently optimistic that I have very few memories of any painful incidents from my childhood. One of them was the year that I was going to be a wolf for Halloween. My age must have been in the high single digits, or maybe I was 10 or 11, when I drew the balderdash reply. I remember the plan: I was allowed to purchase a wolf mask, but the rest of the costume was to be a created by taking a winter coat that had a fake fur lining and turning it inside out so that it could be the wolf's fur.

My pain arose because I wanted to be in costume when the guests arrived for our neighborhood Halloween party, but Maggie hadn't had time to get the coat down from summer storage yet. I remember hiding under the picnic table as she prepared the tub of water, so we could bob for apples, and as she hung decorative items from the nearby apple tree. What was she thinking?

I went to our album of childhood pictures that Maggie gave me in 1987, hoping to have a picture to show you. My year of the wolf was apparently not captured on film, so you'll just have to take my word for it. I was undoubtedly the scariest creature imaginable.

What I did find were some pictures of these neighborhood Halloween celebrations. The costumes are unique, and I can actually only figure a few of them out. Jody has a huge plastic nose attached to the glasses he is wearing, and his face barely shows under Dad's hat. Sheila and Lisa also sport large hats. Whereas Sheila may be a nanny, I'm not sure what type of swashbuckling character Lisa represents. There's no close-up photo of me from this era, but I appear as a devil in the group shots. I include me in my costume when I was about 16 and made my own statement as Daisy Mae, who in turn was dressed up as a witch … a costume on a costume.

Holloween Celebrations
Top Left: Lisa and Sheila; Top Middle: Jody; Top Right: Felix, age 16, as Daisy Mae
Bottom Left: Gypsies and others; The neighborhood kids - Felix as devil

When all of the neighborhood kids got together, the intent of the dress-up was similarly vague. In one photo, Roberta Deering appears to be a gypsy, and there's a fellow taller than Jody who may be a hobo, a popular character to play at the time. The Deerings and Overholts may be able to help me identify the players.

Despite the pain of my wolf incident, I share the love of Halloween that makes it our most popular holiday, even today. Maggie's staunch rejection of the commercialization of the celebration solidifies it in my mind as a cherished memory.

— Felix

NOVEMBER 13, 2011

Dear Family,

This past week, the moon seemed to be full for three nights in a row. For the first two, howling winds blew large clouds dramatically across the sky. On Friday, when I stopped to visit Maggie and Dad, the evening began with a haze almost thick enough to be fog.

I joined them in the living room and shared their evening snack: Black Diamond cheddar cheese and tortilla chips. We watched the progression of the moon as it rose over the river to the east. Dad commented that this was a "Beaver Moon." He is such the master of arcane information that I was compelled to look it up. The Farmer's Almanac has a name for the full moon each month, and Beaver Moon is the name for the November moon. I think only the "Harvest Moon" of September has been retained by the non-native settlers of North America.

At first the moon was murky, rising in the mist just above the opposite shore. When it was well up, it was pretty clear that it was no longer full, given the definite flat spot it displayed at about the 2 o'clock position. It did cast a huge glow on the river, extending the full one or two miles across to Canada.

We looked at it so often that Maggie was reminded of something. She would start to tell me, then get stuck. I tried to guess and finish her thoughts. It took her multiple times before I could piece a story together. I think this is it: When they first moved into the house, she was concerned about how visible they were to people who might be on the water or in front of the house. She decided to put up drapes, but she didn't get around to it until a couple years ago.

I was interested in two things: how determined she was to tell the story, and how she just couldn't piece it together by herself.

Maggie has always been a storyteller. Even with advanced Alzheimer's disease, she still wants to fill that role. I read something from the field of cognitive neuroscience that might help give some insight. Don't hit that delete key yet, because it may also explain why we tend to gossip and spread stories that are not true. Benedict Carey in the *New York Times*, October 31, 2011[33], summarizes this work in a very accessible article.

The story begins with Dr. Michael Gazzaniga, who teamed up with Dr. Roger Sperry to study a group of patients who had undergone radical surgery to treat uncontrollable seizures. They had a surgery that severed the connections between the left and right hemispheres, and the initial impression was that there were no detectable changes in brain function. Gazzaniga, however, did demonstrate a difference in the action of the left and right hemispheres. At age 25, he hatched the now-familiar understanding that the left brain is key for language and speech, and the right brain excels at visual and motor tasks.

Now at age 70, he has continued his research into split-brain patients. He developed a method to show one thing to the left hemisphere only and another to just the right hemisphere. Then he asked the subjects questions about what they saw. When the question concerned the left hemisphere and the answer required knowing what the right hemisphere had seen (which was impossible since the hemispheres were no longer connected), the subject made up a plausible explanation. The left hemisphere took the information it had and delivered a coherent tale to conscious awareness. Gazzaniga says it happens all the time in daily life; almost everyone has caught himself or herself in the act — overhearing a fragment of gossip, for instance, and filling in the blanks with assumptions. This has led him to call the left-brain narrating system "the interpreter." The interpreter creates the illusion of a meaningful script, as well as a coherent working self. It reconstructs what happened and why, inserting motives or intentions, based on limited and sometimes flawed information.

The science writer, Benedict Carey, observes, "one implication is that we are not who we think we are." We narrate our lives, shading the details and even changing the script retrospectively, depending on the event. The storyteller never stops, except perhaps during deep sleep.

So, Maggie retains her irrepressible urge to tell stories and to provide explanations for events. Unlike the patients who had their brains severed, so that the right hemisphere couldn't communicate with the left, Alzheimer's disease has destroyed the nerve connections to memory units, which would otherwise allow her to complete a thought or to concoct an explanation. Looking back, there was a phase in her an earlier stage of Alzheimer's disease when she could use plausible word substitutions to conceal missing connections. Later, less plausible words were substituted, and now none are available at all.

Maggie in an undated photo, maybe late 1930s

A bright moon on a large expanse of water can give us a sense of awe at the wonder of nature. I hope you share some of my sense of wonder in the study of an even more awesome feat of nature: the human mind.

— Felix

NOVEMBER 28, 2011

Dear Family,

These Maggie Letters intend to salute Maggie's life and to be a vehicle for me to better understand Alzheimer's disease. This is a difficult post on both accounts.

I prefer to think of Maggie in terms of events or images that recall her energy and enthusiasm. One image that comes to mind is from Rondeau Park, our family vacation home in southern Ontario. The water in Lake Erie was frequently very cold, in spite of the relatively southern location and the shallow depth of the water at our beach. Often, the four of us kids waded gingerly into the water on our tiptoes to delay the gradual creep of the cold water up our skinny legs. Maggie knew no such hesitation. She plowed into the water until up to her waist and then dove. She always came up for air with words of reassurance that the water was great, once you got used to it.

In my weekly Tuesday study group, we are reading works by Henri Nouwen, a Dutch theologian and priest who died in 1996.[34] His readings for this week are difficult. Nouwen is a compelling writer, who would rather write (and preach, for that matter) from an emotional basis, rather than as an academic or as an agent for Roman Catholic dogma. His books betray a constant struggle against pervasive unhappiness in his life because of his difficulty in finding the right expression for his ministry, his repressed sexuality, and his personal experiences with vulnerability.

This week we are reading about end-of-life issues. Nouwen's point is that our lives will bear fruit at the time we become dependent. This is counter-intuitive, of course, that individuals who are so accustomed to success and to productivity should value the time when they are dependent, something we usually associate with uselessness and as being burdensome.

He urges us to avoid the standard view, which is that success counts, not fruitfulness — and especially the fruitfulness that comes through passivity. We try to avoid passivity at all costs, but Nouwen finds it to be the way to salvation. He contends that care for the dying has as its prime goal helping to make the transition from action to passion (passivity), from success to fruitfulness, from wondering how much they can still accomplish to making their very lives a gift for others.

In my experience, none of this seems apropos to Maggie. She gave up her career as a physician to be a stay-at-home mom and take care of us four kids. She was driving us everywhere, long before the notion of a soccer mom. Her fruitfulness was manifested on a daily basis as we were growing up, not at this time of decline in her life. Once we were out of the house, she changed the scope of her activities again and went to work for the Salvation Army.

In the realm of Alzheimer's, Maggie's passivity has reached another milestone. I wasn't able to get to the folk's house for Thanksgiving because of the travel schedule of our family members. I went over there the next day, coming from a short day at work. Sheila was up from Oklahoma, and she and Dad had lunch ready. We sat at the table in the kitchen and had leftovers: turkey, rutabaga, potatoes, raw veggie stuffing and blueberry pie for dessert.

The chairs in the kitchen are arranged so we can all look out on the water. Sheila and I were sitting next to each other, and we talked just about nonstop, laughing a lot. We paused periodically to include Dad in the conversation by looking at him so he would know to lip read, and we included Maggie by making a few direct statements to her. Maggie didn't eat much and turned down the pie with a flat affect.

When lunch was over, I was on the phone to the hospital as I watched Maggie get up from her chair. The back of her dress was completely soaked. This was her second episode of incontinence that day. Sheila said the first had required a major cleanup effort.

Incontinence of the person being cared for is one of the major issues facing caregivers of persons with Alzheimer's and may be the leading reason patients are admitted to a nursing home. Learning to Speak Alzheimer's advises us to ignore accidents and to praise results. The objective is to minimize the patient's embarrassment, shame and apprehension. The "habilitation" offers an opportunity for feelings of success — and dry pants. I'm worried that Maggie is well beyond that stage. I don't know that she was even aware of the accident.

It's interesting how my Sunday church experience interfaces with these observations. This week, Isaiah 64: 1–9[35] refers to the powerful God, who makes nations tremble at His presence, and Isaiah implores God not to be exceedingly angry and not to remember inequity forever. Just after that, Paul reassures the congregation at Corinth (1 Corinthians 1:3-9)[36] that "they are not lacking in any spiritual gifts," and that God will "strengthen you to the end so that you may be blameless." There it is, one of the great conflicts in the Bible: the division between a powerful God and one who is with us in our weakness.

No wonder Nouwen had such ambivalence about the church, especially given his penchant for vulnerability in his interaction with the sick, the poor and the oppressed. Many of us choose a God who is powerful and all knowing, and want this type of God so strongly that we are willing to accept a God who is angry and may remember inequity forever. We also aim for success and productivity, wanting to please God (and others). Nouwen embraces the God who is with us in our frailty and in our passiveness of our last days. He finds fruition in the very dependence that we dread.

As I watched Sheila head off to help Maggie with a change of clothes, it was painful to see a grand woman like Maggie suffering with this manifestation of cognitive decline. It hardly seems like a topic for a letter to friends and family. But, it's the real deal, and it could well influence our decisions as a family as we step up to the question of Maggie's continued care at home, the role any us of might play in it, and the help that Dad may need.

I gave Caroline a sneak preview of Nouwen's writing for this week. She replied that she was sure Nouwen's writing meant something very meaningful to him, which let me know she didn't relate to this topic at all. Both of these are difficult topics, and I'm not writing with the pretense that I have answers. Just some feelings deeply stirred.

— Felix

DECEMBER 4, 2011

Dear Family,

In our crèche, the baby Jesus has already arrived. When our daughter Alison was 4, she said, "My baby Jesus is a girl." For me growing up, ours was always the traditional gender.

This Maggie Letter post has the element of "found objects" that you see in these letters from time to time. We are preparing for a holiday party this coming Friday, so Caroline and I have spent the weekend purchasing and decorating the Christmas tree, putting lights on the outdoor shrubs and getting the house ready. Tonight, we may get the crèche out, which was given to us by Maggie about 30 years ago.

As kids, we gathered every morning around the crèche that Maggie put up. It was made by Mary Catherine out of papier-mâché and bits of plaster. Unlike some versions that are large and a bit crude, these were fine little statues, each hand-painted.

Mary Catherine

Mary Catherine remains an interesting aspect of our childhood. We have never understood her relationship to our family. I'm not even sure how our parents met her. Her husband was a homebuilder in the suburbs of Cincinnati. They were good friends with the Knoops, who published *Reader's Digest*. An interesting sidebar was that the Knoops had such a successful goat farm that they were asked to provide goats for one of Albert Schweitzer's projects in Africa. We loved going to their farm. We associate her with organic gardening, well before its time, and goat milk with coarse raw sugar on our breakfast cereal. The crèche she gave us was rustic, with real straw and convincing animals. We said a morning prayer and opened a door on the advent calendar each day before school.

In contrast to this holy scene, the director of religious education at our church saw the crèche as a chance for some good fun. Diantha Higgins was lively, if not hyperactive, with the skinny frame of a lifetime heavy smoker. When she laughed, it was more like a cackle; her shoulders heaved. She loved to tell how she put up her crèche, but saved the arrival of Jesus for Christmas morning. She said the baby Christ child started out someplace near the kitchen, and he worked his way toward the manger, keeping out of sight of her children, who were dying to spot the babe before he landed. Her kids were known to climb the bookcases looking for him.

Friday, Caroline and I went to the Detroit Institute of Arts to see another version of the search for Christ. The DIA is hosting an exhibit of the paintings and etchings of Rembrandt in which he sought to express his vision of Jesus. The show traces Rembrandt's initial depictions of Christ as a dramatic and muscular man, to those of a more contemplative person. The controversial aspect was his departure from convention to depict Jesus not as a blond-haired northern European, but as a Jew.

Today, our church service was something new to me: an entire service centered on the "O" Antiphons.[37] Fortunately, the service came with a user's guide. An antiphon is a phrase or a sentence from scripture that is sung prior to the psalm in the worship service and is intended to emphasize the central meaning of that psalm. The "O" Antiphons present a name given to Christ in the Old Testament, as in "O come, O come, Emmanuel." The tradition dates to the ninth century and has been attributed to Gregory the Great. The service is one of singing antiphons and reading the scripture on which they are based, and hymns and collects. Collects are stylized prayers that address a theme pertinent to the service, as a collect for Christmas or for the dedication of a church building. The service stands on its own, with no sermon, no liturgy.

The readings have their roots in the same dilemma I addressed in my last post, the conflict between a powerful God and the suffering God who is with us in our weakness and vulnerability. The psalms and scripture selections also take us into the domain of the other great conflict in the Christian life: Do we want to explain God or experience God?

I think it's a "guy thing" to want to explain the world and God. I'm slowly getting the message that the point of the New Testament is that we should forget about rules and explanations, and we should — especially, us guys — just start living the experience. In Mary's words to the angel, "Let it be with me."

Both Maggie and Diantha had it right. There's room for a serious approach and a lighthearted approach. And, in trying to explain the experience, one may miss the point.

— Felix

CHRISTMAS EVE 2011

Dear Family,

Our clan gathered in two cities today. Sheila's family was in Chicago, where her daughter Rose got married to Andreas in the afternoon. Lisa flew in to Chicago for the day, and my nephew Toby's family was in the wedding. The rest of us celebrated Christmas with a brunch at our house. We would have been hosting Caroline's parents, except her father broke his hip last week and couldn't leave Washington, D.C.

We hired a chef to make our life easier, and the guests arrived in waves. Jody and Rosemary arrived on time with their daughters, Lindsey and Rachel. Maggie and Dad got here 45 minutes later. Maggie was wearing a dark blue winter coat and fleece gloves; on her arm, she carried a small leather purse. Beth didn't bring the real celebrity, our grandson, Teddy, until an hour after that.

We started with champagne, in honor of the season, and also since we hadn't been together in such a long time. We opened presents in batches. The cook fell way behind in his preparations, possibly because of the extra time needed to make the gluten-free crust for the quiche. Maggie seemed to be getting tired by the time Beth arrived with Teddy, and she chose not to have him sit on her lap. Dad did a great job in the role of great-grandfather. Somehow, he had found time to buy Christmas presents for all of us.

At brunch, Beth, Lindsey and Rachel dominated the conversation. They are each funny by nature, but all together on a day like this, they are hilarious. At one point, Dad asked for the floor. He speaks so softly that I think some of his comments may have been missed. He started by reminding all of us that Rose and Andreas were probably just married at this point, and the service was likely to be ending soon.

He used that as a transition point to comment on an episode when he and Maggie started dating. He said he knew she was the right person when he began a quote from "The Prophet," by Kahlil Gibran:[38]

"When love beckons to you, follow him/Though his ways are hard and steep."

And Maggie completed the next phrase:

"And when his wings enfold you yield to him/Though the sword hidden among his pinions may wound you."

With that start, he was confident he had found his partner for life.

Maggie watched Dad intently as he spoke. Since he had just obtained the full attention of the whole group, he started again, his eyes fixed on Maggie, and she was looking directly at him,

"When love beckons to you, follow him/Though his ways are hard and steep."

Dad paused, and I think there was a moment of hope in his eyes as he watched to see if Maggie might be able to complete the poem that they had said together so many times over the years. Maggie was attentive but silent.

Dad continued, "And when his wings enfold you yield to him/ Though the sword hidden among his pinions may wound you/And when he speaks to you believe in him/Though his voice may shatter your dreams as the north wind lays waste the garden."

After everyone left, I got out my copy of "The Prophet." I think all of us had a copy when we were in high school, and there was always a copy on the coffee table at home. In the front of my copy was a notecard from Maggie, dated May 24, 1969. She wrote that she didn't write in the frontispiece because of concern that I might already have a copy, and this way we could be economical, as I could send the book on to someone else.

On February 1, they will have been married 68 years. It's so touching to see them live out this love story. The love is deeper and no less intense in the face of Maggie's inability to respond verbally.

Here's the way the section On Love in "The Prophet" ends:

"Love has no other desire but to fulfill itself.
But if you love and must needs have desires, let these be your desires:
To melt and be like a running brook that sings its melody to the night.
To know the pain of too much tenderness.
To be wounded by your own understanding of love;
And to bleed willingly and joyfully.
To wake at dawn with a winged heart and give thanks for another day of
loving;
To rest at the noon hour and meditate love's ecstasy;
To return home at eventide with gratitude;
And then to sleep with a prayer for the beloved in your heart and a song
of praise upon your lips."

"When love beckons to you, follow him."

— Felix

JANUARY 25, 2012

Dear Family,

There was an unexpected change in my schedule today, so I headed to my parents' house before 5 p.m. When I get off work so early, I usually head home and try to make the most of the evening. As we seem to have domestic conflict brewing with my parents, I instead launched myself to Grosse Ile.

Last weekend, I was there to see Maggie and catch up with Lisa, who had driven up from Cleveland for the weekend. The evidence was right in the center of the coffee table: a large, trucker's version of the 2008 Rand McNally Road Atlas. Dad had casually announced that he was going to drive with Maggie on a cross-country trip to Tucson, Arizona, where he and Maggie had lived for about eight years three decades ago. We talked about the trip in general terms, and Lisa and I didn't take his plan seriously.

Over the next two days, it emerged that Dad was completely serious about this venture. He planned to leave on Saturday, February 4, and head due south and then west. He estimated a trip of 2,500 miles. No problem, he said, just 500 miles a day, and he'll be there in five days. They'll stay at the Westward Look, his favorite Tucson hotel.

Sheila, Lisa and I had a burst of email exchanges, many evoking a sense of crisis and girded with a desperate tone. There were only glimpses of the Rogerian humor we usually try to employ at times like this. We pictured a nearly deaf, 91-year-old man driving a 93-year-old woman with advanced Alzheimer's disease. We envisioned the types of catastrophes that could arise, from accidents of incontinence in the car, to wandering away in a new city, or disorientation leading to a complete meltdown. It was agreed that I would reason things out with Dad and persuade him to abandon this plan.

I arrived from work as the folks were seated at dinner. Dad had cooked one of his specialties, baked sweet potato. I don't think there were other items. The dinner looked spartan, if not penitential. As they ate, I brought the trip up from several perspectives, like the length of the journey, expense, isolation, disorientation, anything I could think of.

After they finished eating, Dad and I kept talking, and Maggie cleared the table. As she did, we both watched closely, fearing that she would do something wrong or make a big mess. Her sight may be bad enough now that she scraped the food off the plates onto one dish with her fingers, rather than try to use a utensil for that purpose. Her final task was to clear the water glasses, and she chose the tray used to cook the potatoes to transport them. As she set the tray in an unstable spot next to the sink, we both breathed a sigh of relief since nothing had spilled.

Watching me look at her, Dad commented that he really didn't need to be warned about the difficulties facing them on their trip. "After all," he said, "It's always an adventure here. There's always something." And he began laughing. It was the first real belly laugh I've heard from him in years. And he kept laughing. As Maggie walked by him, he swung his arm out and around her waist the way a man does in an affectionate gesture when he's dating.

He asked if I noticed the cushion on the chair next to mine. He said the one on Maggie's chair was often wet. Today he said it got wet for a different reason. Maggie started to pour a glass of water and just kept pouring, until the pitcher was empty. It was a small pitcher, but it still made a good-size pool of water. Dad laughed another belly laugh. His head rolled back, and his eyes met mine in invitation to join his laughter. I was glad to. He was genuinely happy.

It dawned on me that there were many elements rolled into his plans for this trip. He needs to get some relief from the constant burden of daily care for Maggie, he wants a vacation from work, and he needs some sunshine. Most of all, I think he is craving the chance to be unreserved in his search for happiness. I haven't seen him this excited about a project in years.

So, I hope I don't disappoint my sisters and brother, but I abandoned any attempt to talk him out of the trip. I reassured him that he could always turn back if things weren't working out. He's planning to take the whole month of February for this trip. It will begin just after their 68th wedding anniversary. I think Dad may be seeing this as a cross-country road trip to serve as a replay of their honeymoon.

— Felix

MARCH 23, 2012

Dear Family,

In the last 24 hours, I received so many calls about Maggie's condition that I was preparing myself for the worst when I drove to her house today. They made it out to Arizona and back without any accidents or serious problems. Both Sheila and Lisa dropped what they were doing to act as tour chaperones. Sheila flew to Oklahoma City and drove with them the rest of the way. Lisa flew to Tucson to oversee things, and Sheila flew to Tucson to escort them home. Do you remember the line of Woody Allen, who commented that the lion and the lamb would lie down together at night? But the lamb isn't going to sleep very well! Although my dad may have claimed the trip was a welcome vacation, neither of my sisters got any rest.

Maggie was fine until last week, when she went to the emergency room because of confusion and increased weakness. After a long evaluation, nothing specific was found, and she was sent home about 3 a.m. When I talked to her on the phone last night, she was more distracted than incoherent. There were long pauses in her conversation.

As I approached their house, I rehearsed several possible scenarios, including a father-son talk where Dad and I agreed this was the end of the line. After 93-plus years, if she has had a significant stroke, the treatments that are part of stroke resuscitation are not appropriate for her, given her age and the likelihood of severe and complex cerebrovascular problems that would minimize any chance of success. At the same time, her age and frail status would significantly increase her risk of complications. The best option seemed to be to do nothing. I parked the car to the side of the driveway, so there would be room to get an ambulance in.

Dad had said in his phone call to me today that Maggie just wouldn't wake up. The caregiver had tried to get her to do her regular exercises. When I arrived, Maggie wasn't in bed, but she was on the couch in the living room, slumped backward against a pillow propped behind her back. She looked weak. Her gaze was distant, and her left eyelid drooped more than halfway down over her eye. She had a sandwich of sorts (no discernable meat or other item appeared to be between the slices of bread). She was taking the tiniest bite and chewing constantly. She didn't acknowledge me. Dad said they were having some toast, and asked if I would like some. I opted for green tea.

As we talked, Dad offered his diagnosis: Maggie has been under considerable stress, what with her trip to the ER and then a couple of sleepless nights followed. It reminded him that she had been treated for adrenal insufficiency many years ago. In its full-blown state, the disease is incompatible with life because there are no stress hormones available to maintain blood pressure and vitality, but there seems to be a huge spectrum of illness, and hers would be a state of minimal involvement. Dad had treated her as if this was adrenal insufficiency and had given her a dose of cortisone several hours earlier and another dose just before I got there.

Maggie finished her toast sandwich and the mug of fat-free milk that he offered her. With her right foot, she beat out a rhythm in three-quarter time. She was very regular... tap, tap, pause ... tap, tap, pause. Over and over, until her left foot joined in, then her right hand, then the left. She seemed unaware of this development; her left hand was tapping against my thigh.

I did a quick exam: Her blood pressure, pulse and the cardiac exam were all normal.

Dad asked if she needed to use the bathroom. She nodded almost imperceptibly. He then volunteered me to take her to the bathroom.

It took the two of us to get her to stand. I kicked the coffee table out of the way to have more room. Maggie was walking with tiny, deliberate steps. It took forever to get her to the bathroom, but I was impressed with her ability to walk the distance without going down. If she had suffered a stroke, it hadn't affected her arms or legs. "See if you can get her to sit down on the toilet," he said as he disappeared into the kitchen.

In the bathroom, I noticed that he hadn't taken any advice about altering the house to accommodate her limited mobility. There were no handrails, and the toilet didn't have an extender or arm rests to aid in getting on and off of it. It wasn't elegant, and it seemed odd, even for a dutiful son, but I got Maggie out of her soiled underwear and onto the toilet.

As she sat there, Dad returned, and I opened a new line of conversation. "I spoke to a patient's family last week. There's a small place for assisted living about a mile from here, limited to just six patients. You might consider that for you and Maggie some time." I didn't think he heard me so I repeated it. He said it wouldn't be necessary.

We got her some clean underwear, and then Maggie washed her hands for what seemed forever. I walked her back to her usual chair. She was clearly better. She answered questions and seemed more alert. The cortisone was kicking in. I think Dad had gotten the diagnosis correct, and there was no need for an ambulance, no need for an urgent physician visit, no need for a man-to-man talk.

I directed the conversation to Dad again, reiterating the comments about the residential home for assisted living, repeating it to be sure that he heard it. He said his primary goal was to maintain Maggie's independence, so that might be something for the distant future.

We talked about the medical office and his plans to look for a smaller house or condo. I looked at my watch. I was ready to leave. Dad thanked me for coming. I gave Maggie a goodbye kiss.

As I was leaving, Dad said, "Be sure to give me information about that residential home."

— Felix

NOVEMBER 25, 2012

Dear Family,

It took a sleepless night and a lump in my throat at church this morning to get me to revisit The Maggie Letters.

It's been so long since I have written that it's hard to pick up the thread. In my post of January 25, 2012, I wrote that Dad was planning a trip to Arizona in early February. Those plans were met with strenuous objection. As I mentioned in the last post, Sheila and Lisa acted as chaperones for much of the trip, helping with some of the driving and spending time with them in Tucson.

In March, Dad proved that he is still the master of secretive planning. This time he announced on a Tuesday that he was leaving in two days to head to Florida with Maggie. He returned a couple of weeks later. He said he came back sooner because the weather was too rainy, but cheerfully announced he had found a place to live when he moves to Florida.

He showed us a real estate agent photo of a house in Crystal River, located along central Florida's "Nature's Coast." The house was so dreary that it looked like a place in a trailer court, except it was made out of cement blocks. Sheila and I happened to be there together on a weekend day, and we tried unsuccessfully to convince him it would be a bad decision for him to move to Florida. Among other things, Sheila had just bought a house on Grosse Ile about two miles away, so she could be closer to the folks.

The push to Florida was interrupted when Dad hurt his back trying to lift Maggie. He had spinal epidural injections for that, with minor benefit. But the episode at least convinced him to retire, which he did in May. After the epidural injections, Lisa made arrangements for surgery at Henry Ford Hospital. The surgery itself went well, considering those were brittle, osteoporotic 92-year-old bones that had created serious spinal stenosis and several vertebral body fractures.

Surgery was complicated by Dad's atrial fibrillation and by considerable difficulty in pain control. Afterward, Dad was transferred to a rehabilitation center for two weeks. He objected mightily, complaining about his chemical sensitivities, the lack of organic food, etc. Eventually, he capitulated and spent the weeks there in good spirits. He's now getting around with a cane.

Dad put the house on the market soon after his return from Florida in March. Even though it's a great waterfront property, he didn't get a serious offer until early fall. I'll spare all of the drama about each twist and turn with the real estate showings, the offers and then our attempted "intervention" when we all assembled as a united front to convince Dad to take the house off the market. Although he did do just that on a late

Saturday night call, he reversed all of it a few days later. He closed on the house in November and now has until December 9 to move out. He hasn't figured out how to get to Florida since there is so much opposition to the trip that no one will drive him, he doesn't have a place to move to down there, and he hasn't arranged for caregivers. However, he still doesn't see any barriers to his plan.

He keeps saying that he wants to simplify his life. (We also think he may be short on cash.) So, he announced that he was going to put the entire contents of the house up for auction. The appraised numbers came in very low. We agreed to an interesting version of Thanksgiving: Last night we gathered at his house to walk through and choose those things that had sentimental importance (or artistic value) to us. We each got two items "on the house" and then paid the appraiser's price for the rest of our choices. Although the usual situation would be to inherit those items, we assumed cash was tight, and we should help out. It was arduous. Many of the items had been in the house since before we could remember.

Then we went to Jody and Rosemary's house for dinner. It was a huge effort just to get Maggie and Dad to go the two doors over. It was dark by then, and a cold front had moved in. We drove the very short distance in three cars. We had appetizers and champagne in the kitchen, gathering around the large table in the center of the room. We moved chairs in for the folks to sit on as we put the final touches on the meal. Jody's son Toby was there with his family. Everyone took turns talking to the parents about the planned move to Florida.

At dinner, there was a kids' table in the next room, and the rest of us were in the formal dining room. Dad couldn't hear anything we talked about, and Maggie was clueless. We all talked among ourselves. It wasn't until the next morning that I realized I hadn't asked my nephew or nieces anything about their lives, how my nephew's business was going or how the nieces were doing in school. We have become so focused on this move to Florida, and our inability to dissuade Dad, that we have lost touch with our perspective on the rest of our lives as a family.

Maggie has shown a relentless decline, and now Dad is unrealistic in his plans for the two of them. Although we cannot doubt his love for her, we can't feel that he really has her best interests at heart. As their lives wind down, and as we clear out the home of all that we hold dear, it's fair to ask what we harvest after all this.

Today was the Sunday after Thanksgiving. Besides celebrating the harvest, we acknowledge the end of the church year. Advent starts next week. The readings focus on sowing and reaping, and the Kingdom of God. In the prayers of the people, one line was particularly arresting:

"May [we] receive a rich harvest of love and joy and peace."

Forget the furniture! As my friend, the author Kathe Koja says, "In three days, everything will be covered with cat hairs anyway."

We want that harvest of love and joy and peace.

— Felix

DECEMBER 7, 2012

Dear Family,

I remember when I picked up Cousin Jamie at the airport in Detroit nearly two years ago. She had told me how to spot her, so I could introduce myself to her. We began with the usual sort of opening lines, like, "So how are your parents?" I told her of Maggie's progressive decline and my father's deteriorating hearing compounded by his refusal to wear hearing aids.

Jamie interrupted me, held up her right hand and said, "Let's take a pledge right now that we won't become stubborn when we get older." We had only met one minute before, but of course, I raised my hand right there at baggage claim and took the pledge.

If she referred to a McGown tendency to stubbornness, she missed the important part of our family conflict. My father's stubbornness is legendary and now has taken on Olympian proportions. Dad is irreversibly determined in his plans to head to Florida. He had threatened to leave this coming Thursday. Until now, it was a hollow threat since he had no means of transportation.

We four children have done everything we can think of to convince him to stay. We've tried psychology and reverse psychology, threats and pleas, tears and laughter, sarcasm and flattery, and feigned indifference. When visitors came by last week, he told them that by his count the score was now 22 people against his move and just himself in favor. He savored those odds.

Over this past week, we have developed a host of creative approaches to the topic. One of the best was the idea of Rosemary and Jody's, that they rent an RV to transport them down to Florida. The RV would solve the problem of getting Maggie in and out of a public bathroom, restaurants and might help with the disorientation from constantly changing scenery. Unfortunately, although we argued that position for several days, the potential driver we interviewed needed to give two weeks' notice at work, and Dad wasn't willing to wait that long.

Dad still plans to buy a house as soon as he arrives down South, ignoring our suggestion that he rent until he gets a chance to check out the housing market and to be sure that he enjoys his new life in Florida.

All of us are mystified by Dad's insistence on moving to Florida, away from his family at exactly the time that he and Maggie most need our help. Our paternal grandfather retired to Florida, and that may be part of Dad's motivation.

I also recall a conversation I had with Dad sometime after his trip to Scotland to celebrate his 50th wedding anniversary. He told about meeting Maggie's relative, William Young, the Presbyterian Bishop to Pakistan.[39] Cousin Willie as he was called, was a missionary before entering the church leadership. He told about two men who called on him at home late one night, motivated by the sermon that Willie had given that day. They said, "Tell us more about this God who gives rest to those who travail and are heavy-laden." Dad was impressed that these men had known such hard work all their lives that the one aspect of Christianity that appealed to them the most was this promise of rest.

As I consider the trajectory of Dad's life, I think his decision to work until this past May, when he was 91, may have some impact on his obsession with getting to Florida. He has always worked so hard and deferred many vacations. Now that he is retired and should be relaxing, he has a major role to play in the constant care of Maggie. Although the caregivers are wonderful people who do great work, it's still a constant duty. He does deserve the rest.

For the present, however, Dad is stuck in his home, with no driver to take him to Florida, and he's dug in his heels, rejecting other suggestions that he might just vacation in Florida, or that he might move to a small condo nearby, where his life would be more simple and less stressful. We're all hoping he doesn't take off by himself early one morning.

At one point in these letters, I worried about the genetic traits that I might have in regard to developing Alzheimer's disease in later life. Now there is another worry that arises from the father's side of the family: stubbornness.

Fortunately, I've taken the pledge.

— Felix

DECEMBER 8, 2012

Dear Family,

It fell to me to commit the act of civil disobedience.

I was just minding my own business and returning from the farmer's market this Saturday morning when Sheila called me from Chicago. She told me that the morning caregiver, Molly, had called her. Dad had expressed his concern that the handyman Brian hadn't returned his phone call. "Didn't he know that I might not be here tomorrow since I may leave for Florida in the morning?" Since she also said that the bags are all packed, I had to take this seriously.

The obvious thing to do was to take a pre-emptive measure to be sure that Dad couldn't attempt to leave in the morning. It's hard to think he really could do so since he can't get Maggie in and out of the car. But he might have coerced a caregiver to get her into the car.

Molly and I made our plan. She would leave a set of car keys outside the garage, I would pick them up and drive Dad's car to another location. Molly would follow, and then take me back to the house. It all went smoothly, but both Molly and I commented on how our hearts were racing while we were implementing the plan.

When I got back to the folks' place, there was a stir in the house since Brian and Dad had just noticed that the car was gone. They may have been ready to call the police. When I said that I had taken the car, my dad's response was, "That's good. We can relax now that we know nobody else took it."

We went into the living room. The afternoon caregiver, Sheila Cooper, expecting the worst, asked if I minded if she would close the doors to the kitchen, so the anticipated shouting would carry less to Maggie. I know that an action similar to the one I took has happened in many families and resulted in serious domestic stress and reports of ranting and raving.

There was no explosion. I presented a letter since Dad can't hear well at all now, and I didn't want to risk a misunderstanding. He read the letter without comment and chuckled at the last sentence. In the letter, I told him he could have the car back when he fulfilled these obligations: that he have a driver and caregiver accompany him to Florida, that he have caregivers arranged to meet him there and that he have a clear destination.

Dad did me one better. He said that he would abandon the idea of buying a house in Florida and settle for a fully furnished rental. That would solve a lot of problems. He then asked me to find the rental and the driver/caregiver for him. I told him I would try. He asked me to call the real estate agent on the spot. I called and got his voicemail.

We now have yet another strategy decision. Should we agree to this compromise, knowing it would likely be hard on Maggie to be in such unfamiliar circumstances? Or, should we come up with a series of delaying tactics in the hope that Dad will eventually cave? On the one hand, good medical advice would say not to disrupt Maggie's environment. On the other is the need to acknowledge the resoluteness and determination that Dad has with respect to getting to Florida. An email survey of the kids is pending as this is being written and a conference call may be our fallback action, so we can come to a consensus.

The last sentence, at which Dad had chuckled, was this: "This action is not intended to diminish in any way the enduring love and respect that all of us have for you. We are just concerned for your safety, as well as that of Maggie."

There is much sadness in this confrontation, which creates such a sharp edge in our relationship and ushers in an era in which intervention is now necessary for both parents. Beyond this drama is another insidious issue, that of Dad's gradual detachment and withdrawal from us as he maintains his focus on going to Florida. I guess we need to acknowledge his great need for rest; he has been heavy-laden.

— Felix

A Family Photo Album

Top Left: Maggie and JTR; Top Right: Maggie and Caroline;
Center Left: Joseph Rogers on Father's Day, 2011;
Center Middle: Lord Bentley and Lisa;
Center Right: Mona and her mother, Sheila DeMare;
Bottom Left: Expectant Elizabeth, Rose, Lisa and Maggie;
Bottom Right: Frank DeMare, Lindsey, Jody and Rachel Rogers

THANKSGIVING 2013 AND 2014

The entry of 12/8/13 makes the claim that the photos of my nephew and his family can stack up against the masterpieces from the Mauritshuis Collection that were on display at the Frick Gallery. This is a proud exaggeration, of course. To see the Girl with the Pearl Earring and the other works, go to https://www.frick.org/exhibitions/past/2013/mauritshuis

Left: Vivien, Elijah and Chris Grayson with Dad; Top Right: Elijah Grayson with Dad and Maggie; Bottom Right: Maggie and her great grandson, Elijah

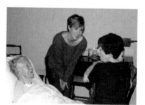

Top Left: Jack was soon engaged with the toy house, and JTR spurred him on;
Top Right: Da Boyz: Jody, his son Toby, and (left to right) grandsons Cameron & Harrison;
Bottom Left: Maggie reached out to Jack with her hand. With help, he grabbed it and held on, but his eyes never left the toy house;
Bottom Right: Maggie follows the conversation and movements in the room, and here watches Alison and Caroline introduce Jack to her.

BASSWOOD LAKE

Top: The walkway at Windhover on a late summer afternoon;
Center Left: Felix, Maggie and JTR on Basswood Lake;
Center Right: Shoreline seen from Basswood Lake, 2014;
Bottom: Caroline and Sharon Hoffman on Melwel Road, October, 2014

SCIENCE

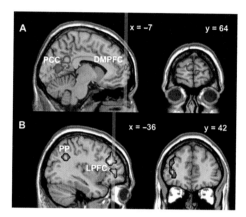

The relative location of the narrative and experiential self-focus conditions in the brain. In panel A, the narrative focus is color coded blue, and is seen in the prefrontal cortex regions and to a lesser degree in the posterior cingulate cortex, a midline structure in the back part of the brain. The experiential focus (I am here) is shown in red in panel B.

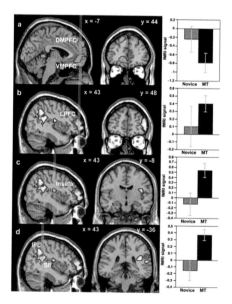

The functional MRI images in terms of the narrative versus the experiential focus. Trained subjects were able to show a greater association with the experiential focus. They demonstrated 2 attributes: they suppressed activity in the narrative area (panel a) by activating the areas of the brain that maintained attention in the present moment and areas that allowed them to suppress the narrative midline structures (panels b-d). The bar graphs show how the subjects who completed an 8 week training program in mindfulness meditation (MT) had more marked changes in each category, with far greater suppression of central cortical areas where daydreaming occurs, and greater activation of the lateral attention centers compared to novices.

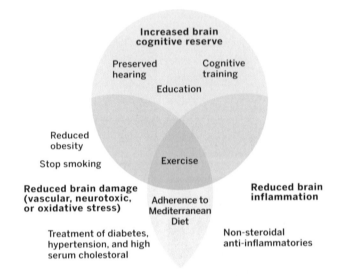

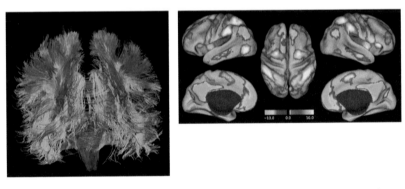

Top: Potential brain mechanisms for preventive strategies in dementia. See ref. 26;

Bottom Left: This isn't "your brain on a bad hair day"... it's a map of the white matter connections from a 73 year old Scottish woman in the research trial. These maps suggest that it's not just the amount of gray matter, but better neuronal wiring in old age that is linked to higher cognitive function. Image: Mark Bastin and Dave Lieward, Brain Research Imaging Centre, University of Edinburgh. (See reference 52. Described in post of December 6, 2015.)

Bottom Right: Images of a normal human brain at rest.
There is highly organized intrinsic brain activity. Described October 10, 2011.
Image: Fox MD, et al. PNAS 2005; 102 (27) 9673-8 (See reference 31)

FAMILY CHRONOLOGY

Top Left: Maggie with Bishop Desmond Tutu,
JTR opens a bottle of 1899 sherry. Maggie, Lisa & Felix look on. Feb, 1994;
Top Right: Dancing at Alison's Wedding, August 21, 2010;
Center Left: Maggie with Tucson artist Ted DeGrazia and JTR;
Center Middle: Maggie with Vivian Overholt;
Center Right: Andrew and Robyn McGown, Bali, 2008;
Bottom: Dad and Sylvia meet, December 10, 2012

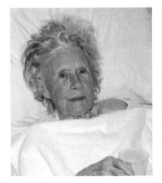

Top Left: Finding the old photos from Kirksville yearbooks.
Jody, Rosemary, Caroline and Jamie. January 29, 2011;
Top Right: Should this man be planning a 2,500 mile car trip?;
Center Left: Maggie at Crystal River, June 2013;
Center Right: Tea time in the home at Crystal River, March 2013;
Bottom Left: Maggie in the subacute rehab center, Crystal River, Florida,
after she fractured her femur. January 20, 2013;
Bottom Right: Maggie and Sylvia

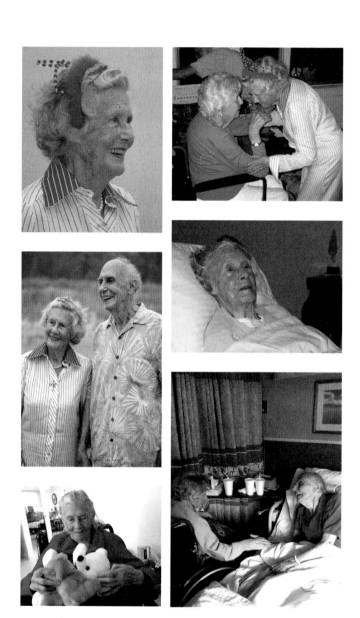

Top Left: Maggie at her 90th birthday celebration;
Top Right: Vivian Overholt, age 94, greets Maggie at her 90th birthday celebration;
Center Left: Maggie and JTR at her 90th birthday celebration;
Center Right: Maggie lying at rest, December 19, 2014;
Bottom Left: Maggie really seems to like the stuffed animals she's been given;
Bottom Right: Maggie visits JTR at the rehab unit in Florida, June 12, 2013

CHAPTER SEVEN

Maggie & Dad Move to Florida

DECEMBER 12, 2012

Dear Family,

Enter: Sylvia.

I would certainly describe Sylvia as confident. She arrived at my parent's house at 8:30 a.m. this morning and joined Maggie and Dad at the breakfast table. Maggie had finished her breakfast and was resting so quietly she had started to doze off. Sylvia engaged Dad in conversation the same way she had two nights before when they were planning this trip. Sylvia had already told us the style she would use with Maggie. She said she would smile at her every time she looked her way. That way, Maggie would know she was friendly. It seemed to work. Sylvia knows her stuff!

It was a quiet, emotion-filled scene in the kitchen. The sun was just up over the Canadian shore, and a large black freighter passed by slowly with the gunnels not far above the water line, heading south with a full cargo. Stephanie and Marcie were there as two caregivers, and Jody and I stopped by before heading to work for the day. The mood was light. Dad's excitement was clear. It seemed to take forever for him to finish his breakfast.

But, if I had to choose just one word to describe Sylvia, it would be "capable."

Which is good, since she left this morning with Maggie and Dad in his big, black Lincoln Town Car. They left about 10 a.m. and made it as far as Corbin, Kentucky. That's 413 miles from Grosse Ile. I had gotten a progress report in the late afternoon, at which time they were hoping to make it to Tennessee, but they settled for an interstate spot just north of the border. At least one person wanted to be a fly on the wall to observe how they did on the drive down. Two dominant personalities, one flamboyant and brassy, the other quiet but relentlessly persistent. When I called at 7 p.m., they were having dinner with room service in a Holiday Inn. Sylvia described Maggie as sitting back with her shoes off, munching her chicken.

Before they left, we had taken a few pictures and then left to head to work, with the last few items remaining for them to put in suitcases and pack the car. All the contents of the house were otherwise untouched. Dad left with everything still in its place — or in its place of disarray, that is, wherever it was last put. All of the kitchen utensils are in place, the dishes are on the shelves, all of the drawers are still full. The closets and dressers are half-full, the tables have piles of papers on them, some of them neat, others destined for the trash. The folks made a pretty clean break.

Jody and I are left with the cleanup, and he seems to be taking most of that on. The packers will arrive in nine days and move the stuff out two days later. By then we should know if this whole thing is going to work and whether the furniture should go into storage or be moved to Florida, or if it's a complete bust and they are on the way back to Michigan. The day they left, Sylvia got up from the table announcing, "I might get to Cincinnati and pull a 'U-ie.'" (That would be a U-turn: to reverse direction, to change course abruptly!)

This event hasn't taken place without significant collateral damage. This is a trip of considerable magnitude, and none of us feels it is wise. We sympathize with Dad for his dearly held vision of retiring to Florida. And we are just as strong in our hope that Maggie is well-cared for. We disagree on strategy and timing, mostly because none of us knows exactly what to do. We haven't faced a situation like this before and don't have a source of authoritative advice. Dad's herculean resolve adds a daunting element. We four kids have butted heads on several aspects of this. And, despite some pointed words, I'm confident we will all emerge as a united family unit, still loving and considerate of one another.

I'll update this as Sylvia sends reports.

— Felix

DECEMBER 14, 2012

Dear Family,

I wish I were a humor writer because I could then put all of this in the best light.

The bottom line is that Sylvia delivered Maggie and Dad to the Best Western motel near Crystal River this afternoon. That's the good news. Everyone got there safe and sound.

There were some rough edges. Sylvia called me last evening. They had made it to Valdosta, Georgia. Dad had made motel reservations a few hundred miles earlier. When they got to the hotel, Dad said they would register and then drop the bags in the rooms. Sylvia took one look at the multiple stairs they would need to climb to get in and out of the rooms and the hills they would need to climb to get to dinner. She dug in her heels and said they would go straight to the restaurant. She and Dad then had a vigorous disagreement, which culminated in Dad saying, "I'm paying you to drive me to Tampa." To which Sylvia replied, "No, you're not. You're paying me to keep you and Maggie safe, and I may just turn this car around and head back home."

Dad accused Sylvia of being confrontational and argumentative. Sylvia returned that he was bullheaded. But, she won that round and they headed in to dinner. Fortunately, they all benefitted from the healing power of a southern meal: fried fish, okra, beans and hush puppies. Maggie ate as if she hadn't eaten for days, and everyone was content.

Today was a different story. Sylvia is a morning person. Dad said they would be up at 8 a.m. and out the door. Just like the day before, they left just before 11:30 a.m. And, Dad likes to stop for lunch at noon. On top of the hour-and-a-half lunch, he had Sylvia stop frequently for his "potty breaks." He wants Maggie to use the bathroom at the same time, whether she needs to or not. She resisted Sylvia mightily. Dad's choice of stopping at McDonald's made her job especially difficult, since the bathrooms are small, and Maggie got frightened when the toilet stall door closed.

Largely because of her frustration at such a slow start, Sylvia didn't spare the horsepower. When I called on her cell phone to review some details about the caregivers, she told me she was going 90 miles an hour. The people in the office didn't believe me, since Sylvia often comes by the office, and she is so notoriously careful with her driving. When I called back to tell her of the arrangements for her plane trip back, she said, "I can't talk now. The police just pulled me over."

That was her first traffic ticket ever. Sylvia assures me that I owe her big time. She will fly back tomorrow, and a professional home care group, the Granny Nannies, will take over the role at noon. Dad is going to meet the real estate agent tomorrow. The agent told Jody that Dad will be buying a house, not renting, as he had promised. Most of the houses have experienced flood damage since they are in the flood plain where the Crystal River meets the Gulf of Mexico. Maybe that's why a good-sized house is in his price range.

At one point today, Jody was on the phone to the real estate agent in Florida, I was setting up details with the Granny Nannies, and Caroline was booking Sylvia's plane ticket. All the while, Jody and I were trying to continue with our patient care duties in the office. At times like this, it's good to remember that frustration is not an option.

Another key point, as Cousin Jamie pointed out in a poignant email to me recently, is that we should not expect any thanks. It's not going to happen. We just do this because they are our parents, and we love them.
— Felix

DECEMBER 24, 2012

Dear Family,

It's Christmas Eve. If timing is everything, why am I working on this Maggie Letter?

When Dad took off for Florida last week, he grabbed Maggie and just walked out the door, leaving food in the fridge, papers on the breakfast table and mail on the desk. There were still clothes in the closet and dressers. He got Sylvia to load his suitcases in the trunk, and away they went.

Maggie and JTR, probably on their wedding day, February 1, 1943

They arrived in Florida last Friday. Dad took the next day off, then went shopping for a house. The real estate agent Steve called to tell me that he found Dad to be the most obsessively single-minded person he had ever met and one of the most difficult to please. Dad needed a house where the previous owner was not a smoker, and one with no carpets, no vinyl floor tile and no linoleum. After Steve found three to choose from, Dad called back to say he wanted it to be completely furnished, so Steve had to start over again.

In the end, Dad bought the first house that he saw and closed on it Friday, one week after he arrived in Florida. It was unfurnished with wall-to-wall carpeting in every room. It apparently has a nice view looking out toward the Gulf of Mexico.

Jody and I have been under such a press of activities at work that we saved most of the cleanup of the house for Thursday night, the day before the movers were to arrive. We recruited the handyman Brian. We all agreed on the ideal circumstances for this type of work: to have a deadline and to be in a bad mood. And we were tired, too. We didn't want to get sentimental as we went from room to room, and we certainly didn't want to save anything that should be tossed out.

The original plan was to set stuff aside for the family, earmark items for a garage sale, donate things to charity and be sure all of the items for Florida were clearly marked. I emptied the smallest closet into a large bag to take to the Salvation Army. It was mostly Maggie's stuff, but I found a navy cashmere scarf with a paisley pattern. I slipped it into the stash of things that I would take home. When I got to the dry cleaner Saturday, I could see it was riddled with moth holes. The woman at the counter couldn't suppress her laughter.

The pantry was all-organic. You certainly would have guessed that, but did you figure on 25- and 50-pound bags of green lentils, quinoa and brown rice to feed a family of two? How about sixteen 24-ounce bottles of ketchup? Or eight bottles of black cherry concentrate? I filled four cardboard boxes by grabbing everything that wasn't opened. I dropped them off for the Baldwin Soup Kitchen the next day. I wish I could have seen their faces. There were 20 bottles of extra virgin olive oil!

So much time was consumed with sorting for charity that we abandoned the idea after a short while. We decided to work in the same room together, to reinforce the plan that if we wavered on saving anything, the other would talk us out if it. We filled a standard-size Dumpster in no time. We piled all kinds of things in there that might otherwise have been saved or recycled: books, filing cabinets, diplomas and medical licenses. The most poignant thing was to see the family pictures that were to be tossed. It seems like one thing for Dad to leave all of us as the holidays approached, and another to leave behind photos of us, as if there were not to be any memories either. I disappeared to my car with a large boxful.

It had rained hard before we started, and there was a steady drizzle as we worked. When the first set of books landed, there was such a splash that we knew there would be no turning back. Anything that hit the Dumpster was soaked.

Toward the end, we got slaphappy. I thought we were through with the den and opened a cabinet to be sure. Ouch. A big shelf of LP record albums. I debated sorting through to see if any were of sufficient interest they should be saved. Here's where the teamwork came in. Jody saw me hesitating and said, "Let's send them all to Florida. Dad can sort down there!" Since we hadn't packed a record player, it seems clear what the outcome will be. I can't think he'll be thrilled. But I did make the observation that the antidote to a single-minded personality is the prankster. Jody had a twinkle in his eye.

The refrigerator brought forth the intriguing aromas one surely does not want at the end of such a long evening. Several of the foods had changed color noticeably. In the freezer, we found a perfectly good banana with just one bite out of it. It was frozen rock hard and very black. Aware of the need to share alike in the great ancestral grab of household contents, I posted this discovery by email. Lisa claimed it immediately.

Was it Gloria Steinem who said, "Always wear clean underwear in case you get in an accident"? Or did all mothers say that? The point here is that one should be wary about the state of their home when they move out. It can say a lot about you. It provides a cross-sectional portrait and a longitudinal view of your life.

This is a sad Christmas Eve for all of us children. Although we haven't lost our parents physically, there is a great separation.

— Felix

DECEMBER 26, 2012

Dear Family,

I'm starting to worry that Jamie's pledge to avoid stubbornness as we get old may not be a sufficient protection. Our parents' trip to Florida leads me to try to understand the factors that may have contributed to Dad's obsessive determination. And, I'm worried that if there is anything worse than generic stubbornness, it's stubbornness fortified by confidence that you are right.

There is much that is impressive about Dad's ambition and drive. He is a self-made man who grew up in West Virginia, the son of the manager of the general store in a coal-mining town. He became a pioneer in the osteopathic profession, leading the way to cardiology practice and education programs that served as a national model.

He has told us that a formative event for him came when he was about 20. Two or three religious men came through Beckley, West Virginia. They were Hindu, as I recall the story. They spent several days with Dad and opened his eyes to a new way of seeing the world. He felt that they taught him esoteric information that he could not have learned any other way.

His household background was receptive to occult ideas. The family was aware of the teachings of Edgar Cayce, and his sister Isabel was considered to be a psychic who participated in spiritualist summer camps, notably the famous Lily Dale in northwest New York. Isabel drew a sketch of a house she had seen in a vision, assuming it would be the place where she and her husband would live. Instead, it matched the house where I grew up on Grosse Ile.

Top Left: JTR takes our lawn mower, the "Black Prince" out for a spin;
Top Right: Dad at the controls of the Hi Lo used at Safe Foods, an organic food business he established in the 1980s;
Bottom Left: JTR navigating our family boat on Rondeau Bay, mid-1950s;
Bottom Right: Dad with Jody and his Buick Roadster, circa 1948

In the 1960s, Dad read a book review of "The Fourth Way" by P.D. Ouspensky.[40] The review reminded him of the esoteric knowledge he learned from the traveling Hindus. Dad bought the book and then everything else written by Ouspensky. By the mid-1960s, he was conducting a weekly workshop on the ideas of the book. The title of the book derives from a consideration that the three standard ways to spiritual growth of the monk, the yogi and the fakir can be superseded by a system of hidden, esoteric knowledge, which Ouspensky called "the fourth way." The key idea is that man needs to become master of himself.

All of us were expected to read Ouspensky. When Caroline "met the parents" before our engagement, Dad asked her if she had read "The Fourth Way." The ideas of self-remembering, avoidance of negative emotions, and defining our aim became litmus tests for our actions as kids and as young adults.

I always assumed that this orientation was an aspect of mysticism. I was surprised to read just the opposite this past summer. Writing in "Meditations on the Tarot,"[41] an expansive text on Christian Hermeticism, the author described Gurdjieff, the teacher of Ouspensky, as "deprived of all mystical sense." This accusation appears in the 13th letter, an exposition of the tarot card representing death. The author finds the approach of Gurdjieff/Ouspensky to be antithetical to Christian mysticism because it proposes that man can attain a degree of immortality by sheer force of will, by creating friction between yes and no, which leads to a crystallization in the body that will allow the person to survive death. He describes this as effort expended from below and moving upward, analogous to the Tower of Babel, where man attempted to reach heaven by building a massive structure. In contrast, the Christian mystic sets aside his will and opens up to receive the influence of God from above.

It fits that Dad is a proponent of the idea that man can accomplish anything through sheer determination. Much of his life is a testimony to that. But the other aspect of this is its place in the story of the Garden of Eden. God says there, "You shall not eat of the tree of knowledge of good and evil, for on that day when you eat from it you shall die," and the serpent says, "You will not die."[42]

There is so much richness in this short excerpt from Genesis that it can't be fully explored in a Maggie Letter. The pertinent issue here is the conflict between yes and no, and the mindset that results from a deeply held belief that one does indeed have knowledge of good and evil. In other words, that one is right. In many of the other great religions of the world, we have cautions about the need to be right. As just one example, in Buddhism, we are encouraged to approach all things with "beginner's mind."

One of the frustrations of offering this explanation is that I have no idea if I am correct. Dad always sought hidden knowledge not available to the average seeker, and he conceals his thinking well. He might deny all this, even if I have guessed correctly. I offer these ideas just as a guard against that stubbornness that he displays: the combination of a philosophy that says sheer will power is effective, within the context of complete confidence that he is right.

— Felix

JANUARY 11, 2013

Dear Family,

Maggie had another, much more serious fall this week, a fall for which the circumstances were tinged with irony. Dad called Lisa around the first of the year to tell her of his excitement about moving into his new home in Florida. She wrote to all of us to say how happy he has sounded in recent days.

Mom and Dad moved into their new house on Saturday, January 5, 2013. The next day, Maggie fell while trying to walk unassisted out to the front porch. The local handyman, Nathan, had just taken out the three steps that led from the entrance hall down to the porch and installed a gentle ramp. She slipped at the bottom of the ramp and injured her right leg. She was taken by ambulance to Seven Rivers Regional Medical Center.

Nathan drove Dad to the hospital emergency room. There, X-rays showed a fracture to her right femur, the large leg bone that joins the hip to the knee. She had surgery the next day, involving the insertion of a long rod to stabilize the bone. Everything went well. I've since been told that if you need orthopedic surgery, Florida and Colorado are great places for it, in the first case because it's so routine and, in the second, because the population of snow skiers provides a steady source of patients.

It's embarrassing to comment that one of our first reactions here in Michigan was that this couldn't have come at a worse time. Jody is down in Grand Cayman with his family, Sheila is visiting her family in the Chicago area, Lisa has an unprecedented clinical load with no professional support, and my own practice is short-staffed with my brother out and others gone because of the holiday schedule. How can we find ourselves in a position that none of us can drop what we are doing to fly down to Florida to be with our parents? None of us wants to say it, but this is one of the things we feared most when they made this move that we all considered so ill advised. I'm on call this weekend, so I'll plan to go down next week.

Over the last few days, we've each had a chance to have more contact with the caregivers who have been attending to Maggie and Dad initially at the Best Western and now in the new house. They've been great and a real help with transportation, taking Dad to the hospital to see Maggie each day.

Being in contact with the caregivers has also let us learn some disturbing information. Dad has had worsening of his back pain, and yet he may not keep the appointment they made for him with an orthopedic consultant. He hasn't had his blood thinner test (PT-INR) for Coumadin in weeks. This was also the first time we learned that the caregivers are not staying 24 hours. They arrive about 8 in the morning and leave after the evening meal. Today, I learned that Dad has now fallen twice in the last 10 days. He really should be in a secure-care environment, either 24-hour care at his house or in a nursing home. I'll re-enforce the first option each time I talk with him.

We are trying to find out more information about Dad's plans for Maggie after she leaves the hospital. We hope she will go to a rehabilitation unit and not just a nursing home. The Granny Nannies recommend that several things be done to make the house safer when she gets home, but Dad's not keen on those.

I talked with Dad today about 5 p.m., and then talked with Helen Lutes, the caregiver with whom I have spoken before. She told me about Dad's fall. He hasn't had his PT-INR checked yet, but he vows to do it tomorrow. Dad was the one to suggest that I talk with Helen, so I guess he may have wanted her to tell me about the fall. She told me about her concern that Dad should have a person there at night. She said he gets up twice each night and has problems with balance.

I leave Friday morning, the 18th, for Tampa. I should get to Dad's place about 3 p.m. I agreed to meet with Helen then.

— Felix

JANUARY 20, 2013

Dear Family,

Once I cleared the congestion around the Tampa airport, the northbound Florida Tollway was clear and wide open. It was meticulously maintained. There are no billboards. A bike path to the side weaves in and out of sight for most of the way. In contrast, for its 12 miles, Route 98, the road to Crystal River, is a broad boulevard of modern strip malls interspersed with Dollar stores, antique shops, used car lots and other relics of another era. Fat Daddy's Road House, a doublewide whose patio is wrapped in clear plastic this time of year, was unpretentiously welcoming. There's live music there most nights.

The outskirts of Crystal River are more stately with live oak trees draped in lazy clumps of Spanish moss. Turning off onto Fort Island Trail, the terrain changes quickly, becoming the tidal marsh area of west Florida. Dad's subdivision is at the end of a promontory that is surrounded by large mats of black needle rush, a thin sedge about 2 feet tall and dull brown this time of year. The few trees in the area have proven their ability to survive both floods and fires. I saw enough scorched trunks to believe it.

A trail for birders heads off to the left at the start of West Dixie Shores Road. In marsh territory like this, there are plenty of wading birds; I also saw banded kingfishers, osprey, pelicans and ducks. I was on the lookout for the local bobcat (Felis rufus), but I didn't see "hide nor hoof," to use one of Maggie's whimsical phrases.

The folks have a place facing north, on the crest of a dead-end street that curves gently along a tidal stream. The house is just 30 feet from the water's edge. When I arrived, the low tide and wind had conspired to drop the water level so low the streambed was almost dry. In the distance, a nuclear power plant retains its cooling towers, even though it is decommissioned. Three adjacent chimneys pour white smoke into the air, which is caught in the brisk wind.

Dad's house is light and airy, with lots of windows. The first thing he did was to pull up all the wall-to-wall carpeting, except in the two guest bedrooms. His neighbor Nathan put down ceramic tile in several rooms, and he left the terrazzo floor in the kitchen and Florida room. In the last month, the caregivers have managed to unpack nearly half of the moving boxes.

Although most of the unopened boxes are tucked away in the garage or back bedroom, there is still clutter. The place has the mark of a bachelor pad, that of a 92-year-old one at that. Dad needed to push aside letters, pillboxes and a variety of other junk to make room for my placemat at dinner.

When I arrived Friday at 3 p.m., I had a brief meeting with Helen, one of the Granny Nanny caregivers. She is really sweet, with a New Jersey accent. Dad and I then drove to the nursing home. Many of the residents cluster at the front door, either to greet family, to be first in line for the adjacent dining room or just to be where the action is.

Maggie was dozing in bed when we got there. Her TV played a cartoon show at high volume while her nonverbal 97-year-old roommate, seriously contracted from a longstanding palsy, had a faux Roman Empire Christian drama on at even higher volume. Her family spoke over the noise.

Maggie was glad to see me, and we had a long, extended visit. Dad and I returned the next day, arriving just in time to see her at work in occupational therapy. She was unable to grasp the idea of sliding a plastic plate along a curved tube. She did better with attaching clothespins to a metal bar. At lunch, Maggie refused to eat anything. Dad tried to reason with her, emphasizing the need to eat so she would be strong enough to come home. Nothing worked. Maggie was as polite as she was determined. She just repeated "No, thanks," over and over. I've proven myself to be completely incompetent in all three of the languages I studied in college and beyond, but I did read "Learning to Speak Alzheimer's." Logic doesn't work when things are this far gone. I just sat with her until Dad gave up, then we went home. When we returned at dinnertime, Maggie ate everything with relish.

My siblings and I have noticed how slow-paced things are with the parents and how much time is consumed by what little gets done. This trip was no exception. I tried to get some shopping done but spent too much time driving around because of vague directions. On Saturday, I tried to get Maggie's organ working. The movers had just dumped it in the van, so pipes had fallen out of position, the blower had become disconnected and nothing worked. I figured a lot out and got all but one of the keys to work. It needs tuning badly, and I couldn't help with that. For someone who loves music, I'm surprisingly close to tone deaf.

Dad has assembled a team of people to help him get settled in. Nathan, the neighbor down the street has a father who just entered hospice because of residual changes from a stroke. He's sympathetic, talented in remodeling and very nice. Dad gets no shortage of advice

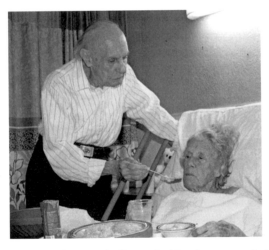

Dad's love, kindness, and affection for Maggie are remarkable.
This Florida home is likely his gift to her.

from his caregivers, especially Bea, who stopped by to feed Maggie this morning as she came to the house on her way to her other job. He faces the challenge of finding household things in different spots each time the caregivers change shifts.

When my visit ended, I called home from the Tampa airport. The tone in Caroline's voice made it clear something was wrong. It was our cat Figaro, who, while I was away, had continued his recent behavior of using our fine Oriental rugs as his litter box. We've battled this for a few years, but now his indiscretions have become more common and involve more areas of the house. Caroline had made the decision to have Figgie put down, knowing that I would agree. In the airport terminal, I sobbed. Choked with tears, I was unable to speak on the phone.

As I thought more about this, I thought it likely that my reaction was more extreme because of this weekend and my experiences with my parents. I did love that crazy cat, but my response seemed extreme. I didn't think it had so much to do with the sanctity of life, since Figaro couldn't even recognize himself in the mirror. No, it was more about his innocence, vulnerability and unknowing. And, it was the loss of affection and companionship that had me upset. We had a routine every morning, when he wanted to be picked up on my lap for a snuggle as I was getting my clothes on. I think it was as important to him as it was for me.

And it made me think of Maggie, who is long past drawing on any past experiences or memories when I come to visit. The caregivers at the nursing home told me how much she loves to hug her teddy bear, which was given to her as part of a promotional event at the local Ford dealership. I've lost so much in terms of being able to communicate with words when I'm with Maggie. She loves to sit and hold hands.

I've watched short-term, then long-term memory disappear. I've seen the loss of control of basic bodily function, and I've observed the deterioration of functional status with each of Maggie's injuries. Her love and need for affection persists, is deep seated, and, I suspect, permanent. Isn't it fortunate, that of all the things that are lost with dementia, love and affection seem to be the last to go?

— Felix

CHAPTER EIGHT

Disaster and Rescue

MARCH 17, 2013

Dear Family,

Maggie wasn't often called on to speak in public. When it happened, she was typically self-effacing and usually witty. When she followed others at the podium, one of her favorite lines was to complain that she didn't have much to say "because the other speakers had used all the good words." We liked that.

The other day I heard a phrase I wish I could use apart from these letters. At a particularly low point in his life, Beethoven was granted an audience with the man he admired the most in Europe, the poet Johann Wolfgang von Goethe. Apparently, the meeting went well. Goethe later described Beethoven as "a lofty misfit." What a great phrase to describe my father, even if these words have already been taken.

The venture in Crystal River, Florida, is not going well, despite Dad's high hopes. Each of us four children has had the chance to spend some time there. The reports describe progressively deteriorating conditions. It's more than just our penchant for filtering the world through our own perspective. When I was there, Maggie was still in the subacute rehab unit, and there were no other distractions for Dad. The pace was slow, and life was relatively calm. Maggie has been home for about a month now and was there when Sheila and Lisa each went to visit. The care burdens are high.

Maggie has slipped a lot in the last few months. Some days the caregivers just can't get her out of bed. She has stopped feeding herself, and the caregivers sometimes need more than an hour to feed her. When I call on the phone, most of the time I hear the voices in the background coaching Maggie to say hello, but she apparently doesn't grasp the idea of the telephone and sits silently with it until I give up on attempts to communicate. Dad has such severe back pain that his activities are restricted to going from one chair to the next. He needs physical therapy but can't drive himself. It will take an extra caregiver in the home to drive him to PT while another stays behind with Maggie.

For his part, Dad is holding firm to his philosophy that structure is good for everyone. He wants Maggie up early with him every day, wants her at the table with meals for him and insists on teatime every day at 4 p.m. A photograph in the album shows a picture that Sheila took on her telephone about February 22, 2013. The folks are pictured at teatime. You will note that Maggie is in a wheelchair. Behind her you can see two additional walkers. This place on the water more resembles a rehab unit than a retirement home.

The caregivers are a great bunch, all from the professional agency that goes by the name Granny Nannies. They are getting tired of what they see to be Dad's unceasing demands. He wants his meals all cooked from scratch with organic ingredients, for example. They consider it excessive to serve tea at 4 p.m. and then immediately turn to dinner preparation.

My opinion, which has not been supported by my siblings, is that this Florida venture is my father's last gift to Maggie. The problem is that he never did get the gift-giving part right. Maggie had a remarkable ability to find just the right gift for anybody. She had a closet with all sorts of knickknacks and souvenirs. A person might stop by unexpectedly. At the end of the visit, Maggie would head to this closet and pull out an item that was just the right thing for the guest.

Most men discover early on in a relationship what makes for a good gift. As other men, Dad had his share of getting things like a whistling teakettle for her, but in his defense, I don't think he ever bought her an iron. Typically, he wouldn't get Maggie anything for her birthday, Christmas or wedding anniversary. Instead, he would arrange an elaborate gift at dramatic intervals, like the time he took his parents and all of us on a four-month trip around the world. He told us that he planned this trip as a break from all the stress in her life that may have accrued from practicing medicine while raising four children who had just reached the age when they all needed to be driven somewhere every day. Many years later, we wondered if she might have had what was later called a nervous breakdown. His folks turned out to be an unforeseen source of aggravation on this trip, and it may not have met its goal.

I think Dad feels that Maggie has lost so much in cognitive skills that she really can't appreciate material gifts, fine meals out, visiting with friends or going to the movies. I think he hopes that she can appreciate the serene life of Florida with just the two of them together. While it may sound lofty, the stark reality is that the two of them are just barely coping.

We are now in the early stages of a rescue plan. We have divided up the responsibilities to look into alternative care arrangements in Florida and in the downriver Detroit area. We anticipate that the conditions in Crystal River will continue to deteriorate over the next few weeks. Then, Dad may be willing to admit that this grand experiment has run its course, and hopefully, he will accept our help.

— Felix

APRIL 25, 2013

Dear Family,

My sister Sheila snapped a picture of the folks' house yesterday morning. The demolition equipment sits in front of the rubble that used to be our parents' house. The day is cloudy and bleak, so there is no horizon, no sky. Just gray.

We were all in high school when Mom and Dad first told us that you can never return home again. I can't recall the occasion that motivated that, but Maggie, in particular, emphasized the point. In 1975, after we were all out of the house, they moved to West Virginia, where Dad took the position of founding dean of the West Virginia School of Osteopathic Medicine. Shortly after, they moved to Tucson, Arizona, where they stayed until the early 1980s, when they did indeed return home to Grosse Ile. When they returned, they moved into the home that I have described in these Maggie Letters, most recently to tell about how Jody and I cleared out the house the night before the movers arrived.

When I passed this photo around the office, everybody agreed that there was no reason to let the folks know their house is now a teardown. The main person of interest would be Brian, the very talented handyman, who got the house ready to sell, working late night after night at the end of his own regular work day, replacing windows, installing fans, rewiring the garage after he put a new door on it and other such tasks. He's often working as a handyman at the next-door neighbor's house, so it's certain he has seen this up close. I have to think he is disappointed since he had invested a lot of emotional energy in the work he did for the folks.

Meanwhile, it sounds as if things have settled into a workable pattern for Dad and Maggie in Crystal River. I think Dad is pleased to hear about the winter that just won't quit here in Detroit. We have hopes for normal spring-like temperatures this weekend, but it's been cold and dreary, just the weather he sought to escape. Each of us four kids has been down to visit, and Jody just returned from his second trip. This visit was motivated by a desire to clarify some issues related to his position as power of attorney and to learn how things stand from a financial point. We are all concerned about this because Dad has 24-hour in-home care and is using a professional agency, which further increases the rate at which he is burning through his financial reserves. We suspect that one day we'll each get a call, asking for a quick ten grand to see him through to the end of the month.

Jody finally brought up these financial concerns with Dad at his recent visit. To be sure that there was no miscommunication, he wrote a note, not trusting Dad's hearing. He asked Dad if things were OK financially and if he had sufficient resources. Dad apparently set the note aside, looked Jody in the eye and said, "You'll be the first to know." Conversation over.

In an effort to keep the topic alive, I called today to discuss this. Dad told me he has enough cash for at least a few more months, and he appreciated my concern, which he will keep in mind. I asked if he might consider a mortgage on the house to raise funds for the expenses, and he said, "That's interesting." Second conversation over.

　　— Felix

JUNE 2, 2013

Dear Family,

I called to speak with Maggie yesterday. Linda, one of the Granny Nannies, answered the phone. She seemed sweet and considerate. She said she would hand the phone to Maggie, and then talk with me afterward. I heard when the phone was placed in Maggie's hand, and I said hello. There was no response. I repeated my greeting at twice the volume. Still no answer, so I did what I usually do: I assumed Maggie was able to listen and recognize that it was me calling. I brought her up to date on all kinds of things. A minute or so later, Linda came on the line. She said Maggie just handed the phone back to her, without a word. Linda said Maggie seems to understand what she says to her, but she rarely says anything more than yes or no or "Ouch!" if something hurts.

Maggie is at home by herself. Dad fell at home about three weeks ago and broke his hip. Actually, the fracture was not of the leg bone where it inserts into the hip joint but in the hip socket itself. That's a pelvic fracture and much more complicated to treat surgically. He was immediately transferred from the regional hospital in Crystal River to Tampa General, a major medical center for orthopedic care. He declined surgery, and the surgeons weren't eager to do it anyway. However, his course wasn't straightforward. He had problems with his heart rhythm, his blood pressure was out of control and he needed blood transfusions, but most seriously, he had problems swallowing. A consideration has been that he had a brainstem stroke, which might have precipitated the fall, and led to his problem with swallowing. He has averted a feeding tube so far. He was transferred back to the same rehab unit where Maggie was, and he will be starting therapy next week.

These are stressful times for all of us. They are time consuming and emotionally demanding. With all of these things, I felt a bit glum on my ride to my local church this morning. Fortunately, today was our annual Kirkin' o' the Tartan celebration. This seems to be a North American tradition, but it owes its origin to A.D. 563, when St. Columba discovered the Isle of Iona in Scotland and converted the previously pagan Picts to Christianity. Over the years, the tradition developed to observe an annual Sunday Tartan Service, when the parishioners would wear their dress kilts and rededicate themselves to the Heavenly Father.

I'm always impressed that it's a bit like St. Patrick's Day, when everyone is Irish for the day. The church was packed, and the St. Andrews Society Pipe Band filled the place with sound.

Our choir started the service with "Loch Lomond," in an arrangement by Vaughn Williams. So many memories came flooding back. Chronologically, the first was in 1961 when we all visited Scotland. Dad drove us about in a 10-passenger van. We went to Loch Lomond with Maggie's relatives, whom we called Auntie Anna, Auntie Tottie and Auntie Mabel. I remember that we kids wanted to see the Loch Ness monster and wondered why this lake was chosen instead. My diary entry records that we had lunch at the Loch Lomond Hotel and then drove to the lake for tea. The photo was taken of us trying out the latest advance, a "volcano," which was a device to make tea outdoors, boiling the water in just six minutes.

Tea time on the banks of Loch Lomond

The second memory was of a time when my immediate family adopted the first line of the chorus to "Loch Lomond." During one of our happiest vacation times, each day we walked to the lodge for breakfast from our cabin in northern Ontario along a forest trail to the main dining room. Beth and Alison were about 10 and 6 years old, respectively. At each fork in the trail, we sang, "O, you take the high road, and I'll take the low road, and I'll be in Scotland afore ye." We had no idea of the sad outcome in the original song.

Presently, I remember the song best from a recording by Chanticleer, which we have listened to countless times on our trips to Canada. I remember Maggie singing along once, long after her ability to maintain a conversation had fallen away.

The transformation of my glum attitude to one of fond remembrances and then to happiness was a reminder that it often is a decision to be happy. There are many things out of our control, but we can choose to be in a good mood. And, the "amazing grace" (as the pipers played later) is that happiness can also settle on us when we least expect it, but may be in need of it most. These are tough times in our family, and we are all working to be of good cheer. It is so clear that the move to Florida was a serious mistake, and it's taking its toll on all of us — parents and kids, alike.

— Felix

JUNE 15, 2013

Dear Family,

We are having a difficult time with our parents, due in large part from attempting to manage things from a distance. In the six months since the folks left for Florida, they bought a house, Maggie fell and broke her right femur, and Dad fell and broke the part of his pelvis that contains the hip socket itself. In those six months, they have been separated for at least two of them, with one or the other of them in the hospital or a rehab center.

The other issue that bothers us is the lack of a clear-cut medical plan for either of the parents. The physician in charge at the rehab unit still hasn't developed a plan for Dad's rehab. The latest is that he wants Dad to see a local orthopedic surgeon to learn his prospects for bearing weight on his injured side.

Over the course of a few months, we have developed a separation of responsibilities. Jody is the durable power of attorney, Sheila is dealing with the caregivers, Lisa is the point person to discuss the medical issues with the physicians, and I feel like I'm watching over things helplessly.

Our concern is to define the best way forward. One path is clear: If Dad needs surgery, it would be so complex and risky that we would insist that he return to Detroit. The choice is less clear if he can solve his problem with physical therapy. Then the question is whether he does rehab for one or two months and returns to his house in Crystal River, or if he comes home to Grosse Ile with Maggie.

Another concern is an insidious problem that has developed with Maggie. After she had recovered from her broken leg, she was resistant to efforts to help her get up and walk. The caregivers have resorted to just picking her up and putting her in the wheelchair, where she spends the day. Because of prolonged time in the seated position, she has developed contractures — the permanent shortening of a muscle or joint — at her hips and knees, and has lost mobility of those joints. As a result, it seems likely that she will never walk again.

Contractures are a dreaded complication of orthopedic surgery. Although they occur from weakness and loss of motion of the limb, the logical treatment of stretching is of no value. Instead, the treatment is complicated. Among other things, it calls for strengthening of the muscles opposite the involved muscles, something unlikely to be accomplished when the patient has such advanced dementia. The other treatments are unlikely to be done in a home-based setting.

Some time ago (on December 5, 2010), I wrote about the gradual transitions, which I called the soft edges, that characterize the decline of elderly people. This development of contractures occurred without anyone noticing, perhaps, in part, because the folks were not getting regular medical attention. One of the Granny Nanny caregivers took pictures of Maggie at home last week. In them you can see that she looks just fine. However, the loss of mobility carries an ominous prognosis, in this case made worse by the fact that it's unlikely that condition can be reversed.

This decline has occurred because of a series of small losses. But there have been some small victories. On Wednesday, the Granny Nannies arranged for Maggie to be transported by car to the rehab unit, so she could see Dad. Apparently, they just picked her up and put her down on the front seat of the car and then transferred her to a wheelchair when they arrived.

We all share some ambivalence about the best strategy. If they do have a limited amount of time left and they are happy in Florida, maybe they should just stay. We find it heartbreaking that Dad has chosen to be 1,200 miles away from his family. If we were to coerce him into returning and don't really have much more to offer in terms of medical care, we may just increase his unhappiness. Our concern involves Maggie, who doesn't have any other advocate besides Dad, who is doing his best.

— Felix

JUNE 29, 2013

Dear Family,

Sheila flew to Crystal River to help the folks get home.

I slipped into Room 193 on the hospital observation unit mid-morning on Thursday. Maggie was "sleeping like a champion," in the words of her nurse, Cynthia. And no wonder. She and Dad flew up on an air ambulance from Florida on Tuesday. I'm sure just getting them out the door of their home in Crystal River was stressful enough. They arrived at the small airport on Grosse Ile about 2 p.m. Only one of the two medical transport vans arrived to meet them. Since Dad had already been accepted into Belle Fountain, the rehab/nursing center, he took that to Riverview.

The pilot must have suppressed any tendency for chivalry because he announced that he needed to get the plane back to Florida. They taxied and took off, leaving Sheila, Jody and Maggie on the tarmac in a soft, drizzling rain. Since there is no terminal at the airport, they waited for the Grosse Ile rescue squad, who took them to Southshore Hospital. By the time Maggie completed the physical exam, X-ray and blood tests needed for her admission to Belle Fountain, the admitting office at the nursing home had closed. She spent that night in the emergency room. The next day, no female bed was available, so she had to spend that night in the hospital observation unit.

When I walked into her room, it was the first time I had seen her since my trip to Florida in January. My first reaction was that she had lost weight. Her face was so thin she looked like the stereotype of a very old, frail woman. And that she is, but she's also my mom, and part of me refuses to see her like that. I keep creating an overlay of images and memories that imbue her with the youthful vigor and charm of her earlier years.

She was deeply asleep and did not waken when I called her name. I watched her breathing pattern, switching back and forth in my perspective from that of a physician evaluating the condition of a patient to a son just glad to see his mom again. In the former role, I watched her breathing to see if she had Cheyne-Stokes respiration, a cyclic pattern of a series of shallow breaths, followed by deep breaths. The pattern can occur with heart failure and generalized deterioration in brain function. I thought she had the pattern for a while because she moved her arms and her right leg more during the deep breathing phase, but it wasn't sustained enough to make the call.

In the role of son, I observed how very quiet it was in the room. The hospital deserves credit for their noise-reduction campaigns over the years. With no TV or radio, it was a good chance for me to have some reflective quiet time of my own, which I've needed. I softened my observation about her thin face and greatly aged appearance. I saw again the resolute, firm jaw and mouth and was impressed at her quiet dignity of the moment.

This contrasted with my father's experience the night before in Belle Fountain. I was sitting at my father's side in the rehab unit. An ambulance crew delivered Dad's new roommate by wheelchair. Without any acknowledgement of us in the room, the attendant flipped on the TV, turned up the volume and then got the new patient out of his wheelchair.

As soon as he was in the bed, the attendant cranked the TV up further. It had been difficult to shout loud enough for Dad to hear me before their arrival, but then all conversation became fruitless.

Maggie was transferred to Belle Fountain the next day, and it's been great to see both the parents together at last. It's still too early to assess how they are overall, but they seem to have improved in the few days that they've been here. Dad has taken on an attitude of full cooperation. He's willing to wear the portable headset to amplify voices, and he's asked Sheila to make arrangements to be tested for hearing aids. He says he is diligent about the physical therapy.

Maggie has shown the most improvement. Her only response to me on the observation unit was a single nod of the head. She slept most of the day, but she did wake up in time for Sheila and me to feed her some ice cream. Later that evening, she said a few words, and Sheila sent a text message that she was talking more the next evening.

I think all of us siblings move back and forth between a professional, objective perspective and a personal, emotional bond. All of us are emotionally exhausted since it was such a tough time when they were having so many problems in Florida, so I think it is natural that we buffer our emotions by keeping a distance from things. Every now and then, we are caught with our guard down. Yesterday, Sheila told me about giving Maggie a straw at her lunchtime. Making the assumption that she could hear and understand her, even though she didn't talk, Sheila commented on what a treat it was for us as kids to have straws with our meals. She recalled how we had so much fun that we loved to blow bubbles in our milk, until it bubbled all over the glass onto the table. Maggie laughed at this. She was able to understand and seemed to remember this event from years ago.

When Sheila recounted this to me, she caught herself off guard and burst into tears. I've had a similar reaction many times.

We still have a long way to go. The physical therapy physician predicted that Dad may need two months of therapy before he can do any weight bearing on his bad leg. We still need a decision about where they should go for their long-term care. We're all hoping that he will be able walk again, so that we might be able to get them into a more residential setting.

    — Felix

JULY 7, 2013

Dear Family,

A couple days ago, I stopped by to see my parents at Belle Fountain, the nursing home/rehab center. Dad wasn't in his room, but Maggie was in hers, lying on her left side, tapping her right thigh with her hand. Tap, tap, tap … tap, tap, tap, the same rhythmic sequence that she started about two years ago. Maggie seemed to notice that I came in the room. I pulled an armchair up to the bed. She then tapped, tapped, tapped on my hand and then moved her hand back to her own thigh, tapping again. Shortly after, she tapped the rhythm on the bedrail, then on the armrest of the chair where I was sitting.

A few minutes later, an attendant wheeled Dad into the room, just as Maggie was tapping on my arm. "Isn't that great?" Dad said. "She is so glad to see you." I did think it was true that Maggie knew I was in the room, but I thought his reaction was related to the assumption that she had been tapping my arm exclusively during the time I was at her bedside. Maggie still hasn't uttered a word to me since she came back from Florida, and she didn't speak on this occasion.

The next day, I stopped by at lunchtime. It was just Mom, Dad and me. Lunch hadn't arrived yet, and the noon caregiver, Stephanie, was still on her way to feed Maggie her lunch. The conversation turned to the furniture that was left behind in Florida. You recall the chaos that was part of the trip to Florida last December. Dad wanted to know how we planned to get the furniture back and what we planned for the pipe organ. He had bought the organ for Maggie at least 30 years ago. It was a special commission from Gabriel Kney, one of the premier organ builders in North America, a chamber organ built on the tracker principle. This is a component of authentic baroque music practice, where the keys are connected to the organ pipes by a mechanical action.

Actually, we planned to donate the organ to a nonprofit institution. We obtained a professional opinion on the organ. Although it is a fine musical instrument, its configuration is such that a music department is unlikely to be interested in the piece. Our consultant suggested that we donate the organ, and he even volunteered to help us transport the organ to a recipient in the Detroit area.

Dad asked us to keep the organ for Maggie to play. Maggie sat in her wheelchair at the lunch table, tapping out her rhythm on her knees. I asked if Maggie still played the organ. Dad responded, "Not like she did 20 years ago." I asked if that meant she could still play a melody or read from a hymnbook. Dad responded that "it allowed a major connection to reality for Maggie." Rather than pursue this, Dad chose instead to ask Maggie if she wanted the organ. She seemed to nod her head "yes." A few moments later, as Dad and I discussed where we might put the organ, Maggie placed her hands up on the lunch table. Her arms were parallel, with the hands spread about 6 inches apart, the distance one might choose to place their hands on a keyboard. Tap, tap, tap, she played, using her familiar cadence.

Earlier I resisted Dad's implication that there was meaning in Maggie's tapping on my arm. But could there be any interpretation other than that Maggie did understand our conversation and did want the organ? Since she is wheelchair-bound, she would have to be wheeled up to the organ. Is it reasonable to expect her to actually play? And since she didn't say a word at this lunch conversation, am I correct in inferring that she does want the organ and that the chance to play it would enrich her life?

Early on in my readings about Alzheimer's disease, I learned that a goal is not to mourn what has been lost but to celebrate what remains. For all practical purposes, Maggie has lost her ability to speak. Can she still express herself through music? If she moves into an apartment for her ongoing care, would the neighbors object to some organ practice? We have to assume that it would not be the sound of an accomplished musician.

The occupational therapist is really taken with Maggie, despite her severe limitations and inability to do much at all in therapy. She did tell me that Maggie was able to move some small plastic cones, one at a time, from a small stack over to another area. That seemed to be the extent of her ability to follow directions and complete a task. This organ music would be a several levels of difficulty greater.

I consulted one of the resources that I turn to periodically, "Learning to Speak Alzheimer's." It was no surprise that they didn't address issues like playing the organ for patients who are so far advanced in their cognitive decline. However, it's impossible to pick up that book without finding some passages that offer hope and encouragement to reach out to the patient, to "hear what they are not able to say." I don't know if it's feasible, and it's certainly not practical, but put me down as willing to give it a try.

Meanwhile, my brother-in-law Frank (Sheila's husband) took the lead in moving the furniture – and organ – back to Grosse Ile. He drove down to Crystal River with Sheila and oversaw all the packing and clean up.

— Felix

Dear Family,

Today, Maggie is 95 years old.

When we first saw that she was in the early stages of Alzheimer's disease, we knew there would be an inexorable decline in her condition, that the most we could hope for was some way to slow the progress of the disease. We weren't prepared for the long journey it would involve. Although we never identified the start date of her decline, we can look back on a few milestones. These Maggie Letters began three years ago, when her condition led to physical injury, first the fracture of her left elbow, then the fracture of her right arm a year later. At least five years before that we were adapting our behavior with her to account for her gradual decline in cognitive function. This was most clear when we took time away from work to spend a four-day weekend together, which we tried to do each fall at my vacation home in northern Ontario.

On the occasion of my 50th birthday, 16 years ago, Jody recorded much of the party on videotape. Maggie, who was 79 at the time, was quiet a good deal of that day. But when Jody asked her for a spontaneous description of how she and Dad met in Kirksville, Missouri, she gave a fluent, eloquent rendition of the story, much of which was new to us. When Dad was recently interviewed in Florida by a case worker, he was asked when he first noticed signs of Maggie's cognitive decline. Jody heard him say, "about 25 years ago." She would have been 70 at that time, so it's clear that the numbers don't match, and we don't really have a time of onset of her cognitive decline.

Each stage of her decline was marked by some loss, be it of memory, judgment, emotional reaction, word count or bodily function: first with balance, then stool and urine incontinence, and now immobility and loss of speech.

Since she is essentially nonverbal, it's hard to judge what remains of the Maggie that we have held dear for so many years. One key feature is that she continues to charm people wherever she is. She was just in the hospital observation unit overnight recently, and the following week, a nurse assistant told me that she was completely taken by Maggie, that she had fallen in love with her. Despite being nonverbal, she still manages to communicate something about herself. I think it is her facial expression.

She doesn't sit slack-jawed with a dull look on her face. Instead, her face is held in a firm expression that seems to have a smile.

I was reminded of the central feature of the book, "Peace Is Every Step" by Thich Nhat Hanh.[43] It's a great introduction to Buddhism, a book my spiritual director called "Buddhism for Dummies," in the best sense of the phrase. I know Maggie enjoyed the book years ago.

In teaching an introduction to meditation, Nhat Hanh offers this mantra to go with controlled breathing: "Breathing in, I calm my body. Breathing out, I smile." As he develops this meditation technique, he offers advice later about what to do when there are "knots" that seem to preclude us smiling as a natural motion. In his book of daily readings titled, "Your True Home," his offering for July 15 encouraged us:

> *"When you walk in the hills or in a park or along a riverbank, you can follow your breath with a half-smile blooming on your lips. When you feel tired or irritated, you can lie down with your arms at your sides, allowing all your muscles to relax, maintaining awareness of your breath and your smile. Relaxing in this way is wonderful, and quite refreshing. You will benefit a lot if you practice it several times a day."[44]*

The skeptic in me was reminded of the false smile, that of the Cheshire Cat or the cheesy disingenuous smile that I think of connected to a manipulative personality. I recalled the character in Leo Tolstoy's "Anna Karenina," who smiled his "almond oil smile" on several occasions. To be sure of my reference and to get the exact context of the first time he gave that smile, I started rereading "Anna Karenina" two days ago. I have covered 90 pages but haven't gotten to the scene in the park, where I recall that smile first appearing. I'm surprised by how I missed the central role of the smile in the development of that novel when I first read it many years ago. Count Oblonsky's marital difficulties were worsened because of an inappropriate smile, and Levin is persuaded to propose to Kitty because of the way she smiled at him at the ice rink.

Like Levin, I could be making too much of what is perceived to be a smile (Kitty did turn down his proposal). My evidence is not something I can put in words, any more than Maggie has words at her disposal. I think we all appreciate a resolute look of determination on her face, and I believe I see a half smile there.

— Felix

Dear Family,

We were up at our vacation spot in northern Ontario about the time of Maggie's birthday in mid-July. One day when I returned from running errands, Caroline said that she had received a telephone call with bad news. I immediately ran through a short list of things which could have happened to her parents or to mine. It was a relief to hear her say that it was just that our home had been broken into. All our jewelry was taken. She sat down and wrote out a list of the items that were likely to have been taken. Caroline and I have been married 40 years. We added up 36 things. Pretty close in terms of my approach to Christmas and birthdays. Later I found the receipts for most of the items. I think 90 percent of my gifts were purchased within a 10-day window before her birthday or Christmas. That's a pattern of last-minute shopping. A least I knew what she liked.

The seven-hour car ride home gave me plenty of time to think about this. I remembered the first years of our marriage, when Caroline still did a lot of solo recitals. One of her signature pieces was the "Jewel Song" from Gounod's Faust. She began as if she were fastening an earring, and soon it was clear that the staging intent was to see her from the perspective of a mirror, and to watch a young woman preparing to go out for the evening.

Another perspective emerged from crooner Michael Buble's CD that I listened to in the car. Consider these lines from the classic ballad, "Wonderful Tonight," written by Eric Clapton:

> "*It's late in the evening*
> *She's wondering what clothes to wear.*
> *She puts on her makeup,*
> *And brushes her long blonde hair.*
> *And then she asks me,*
> *Do I look alright?*
> *And I say, 'You look wonderful tonight.'*"

Jewelry is great, but it's not essential, and nothing beats the romantic notion Clapton expressed. This took me back to thinking about my parents again. As their social lives and ability to communicate with words has shrunk, they are spending more time holding hands and just sitting with one another. I'm always getting comments from people at the nursing home about how adorable my parents seem to be.

Meanwhile, we are still struggling to find a place for the folks to go after they leave the nursing home. It's been great for Maggie. With all of the social interaction, she is now talking a lot more. Not that she is putting together sentences, but she is able to follow the thread of a conversation. Sheila Jane has arranged for a caregiver to come to feed her for each of the three meals and that adds to the mix.

On the other hand, Dad is bored, and he is tired of the food. Since he does best with pureed food, everything is about the same: pureed beef, chicken or pork, pureed vegetables and mashed potatoes. The gravy looks daunting. We still can't arrange for them to be together in the same room. There are limitations because of the bathrooms, which need to be shared by two patient rooms. The bathrooms can't be co-ed, even at this stage of their lives, and despite the bathrooms in the hallway being marked as unisex. Most days, Dad asks how we are doing in terms of finding another place for them to stay. I think we have explored every rental place and house for sale on Grosse Ile. Occasionally, he points out that he still owns a place in Florida, and they could return there. I respond, "That's not going to happen," and that line of conversation ends abruptly.

The temptation is to point out that most of this didn't need to have happened. Had they not left their beautiful, single-story home on the waterfront on Grosse Ile to take the ill-fated trip to Florida, they would have saved tens of thousands of dollars and maybe avoided a few broken bones. But to say this would be taking the risk of forcing Dad to feel or admit regret for what he has done.

This idea of regret is addressed in another song on this same Buble CD, a piece that was popularized by Willie Nelson. With both singers, the song is so poignant that another idea emerges as I listen. In "You Were Always on My Mind," the singer mourns the "little things I should have said or done," and rationalizes his inaction by the title phrase of the piece, "but you were always on my mind." There are always things that we could have done differently. To look back on them creates sadness for which there is no solution. In this song, the situation seems to be hopeless, and the relationship is over.

I am convinced the most painful emotion that we can bring to a relationship is that of regret. To me, it's much more deadly than the "sin" religious people worry about. Since our relationships, as a consequence of our human nature, are destined to be incomplete, we might conclude that regret is inevitable. In that context, our task should be to protect one another from regret.

It's an expression of love to say, "You couldn't have done anything differently," or, "What you did wasn't so bad, and I have forgotten it." Faced with regret, we can make the most of the situation by resolving to do a better job of being attentive and by working harder to be more considerate and understanding. And, for most of us, we have years ahead of us to follow through on that intent. But, what if you are almost 93 years old and faced with the inevitability of declining health?

— Felix

CHAPTER NINE

Maggie Enters Hospice

AUGUST 24, 2013

Dear Family,

I always enjoy the chance for some quiet time when we are up at our vacation home in northern Ontario. Sitting on the porch and reading, it becomes clear that the language of crows and ravens is the most complex communication in the animal world up there. Most of us just think of the crow in terms of its familiar "caw, caw, caw" (unless you're British, in which case my reading indicates that the crow says, "car, car, car").

Beyond this, the crow has a whole series of other speech forms. In my terms, the crow also makes a "thunk" sound and what I call a "chortle." Actual ornithologists say they may cluck at the sound of a predator, trill when ready to compete for a prized spot with respect to carrion and beg for mercy from a more dominant member of the species. Crows and ravens can also imitate a host of other sounds and say at least a few human words. Historically, the ravens at the Tower of London tell visitors who stray to "keep to the path." Augustus Caesar routinely purchased ravens that spoke, in part, so he could hear their praise, "the victorious commander."

A recent article in *Science* magazine was devoted to the topic of the brains of birds.[45] Crows and other members of the corvid family, including ravens and blue jays, are among the most intelligent of birds, along with parrots and cockatoos. When I was an undergraduate in college, one of my psychology professors made a bit of a name for himself by studying crow communication. That rudimentary study was based on the idea of counting "caws" as a way of determining location and activity within the flock. The field has advanced dramatically since then. The powerful instruments of functional magnetic resonance imaging (fMRI) and positron emission tomography (PET) scanning have now been reconfigured to study bird cognition and memory.

Crows are attentive and have excellent memories. They don't forget the faces of people who threaten them. When they see that person again, they scold them. And somehow, they communicate who the threatening person is to other crows, so that this person may be harassed by crows who have never seen him or her before. These new imaging techniques show that the parts of the brain which are active when viewing a predator that crows innately fear (like a hawk) are different from those that are active when a crow learns and memorizes the face of a threatening person they've not seen before.

Researchers have detailed sophisticated memories in ravens and jays; tool-manufacturing and reasoning abilities in crows; and complex social skills in many bird species, especially corvids and parrots. Corvids are the most studied. Nicola Clayton from the University of London termed corvids "feathered apes" because they have many of the talents celebrated in the great apes, from toolmaking to social networking. Some corvids even surpassed apes on tests designed to reveal things such as the ability to recognize that others have intentions.

It might seem appropriate to ask two questions at this juncture:

What's the point of this research? After all, one of the U.S. political parties has successfully convinced Congress that no projects of the National Institutes of Health should be funded unless they can document that the research will enhance our economy or will contribute to national security.

And, why is this in a Maggie Letter?

Birds have evolved a rich repertoire of mental abilities as a result of living complex social lives — the same theory proposed as the driving force behind the evolution of primate cognition. American crows, for instance, have complex social lives that might shape their evolution. They mate for life, have extended families, communicate with complex vocalizations, and travel, forage and roost in large social groups. If similar social pressures were shown to drive both avian and primate intelligence, it would be a clear example of convergent evolution. In other words, this research touches on the great ontological question of who we are and how we came to be.

Since the driving force of cognition across all species seems to be social interaction, why do we still do such counterproductive things with our patients and family members with Alzheimer's disease?

Maggie's alertness and speech have improved so much since she got back from Florida. I attribute a lot of it to the familiarity of being back with family, but also with the stimulation from the caregivers that Sheila has hired to feed Maggie three times a day. I'm guessing that there were times when she was in Florida and Dad was in the hospital when the caregivers may have just moved her into the living room and turned on the TV, so she would have some "stimulation" during the day. Throughout the nursing home, nearly every patient has the TV on. My observation is that the staff has turned it on for the patient. It seems to create so much random noise. Seriously impaired patients are routinely wheeled out to sit in front of the nurses as they work. I know it's intended to provide some interesting things for them to observe, but it's not social interaction if no one is talking to them.

It would be great if we were able to say that we have learned from our feathered friends and applied the inspiration from this research to our care for patients with cognitive impairment. There are so many subtle forms of social isolation. Our efforts to care for Maggie make clear how hard it is to be present with her and interact personally since she is so often nonverbal. Even on her good days, she can't maintain much of a conversation. But she looks at me keenly when I visit with her, and she maintains her smile. Her room is quiet and serene. The nurses have finally gotten the point that we don't want her TV on all of the time. It's as if the big old bird said, "Nevermore."

— Felix

SEPTEMBER 29, 2013

Dear Family,

I need to catch you up on a few developments. At the beginning of the month, over the Labor Day weekend, Dad left the rehab/nursing home and moved into Jody's house. A week later, Maggie joined him. Dad's move was triggered by running out of Medicare benefits to pay for his care at Belle Fountain. We couldn't move Maggie out until we completed arrangements for her care, including the bed, Geri-chair and caregivers.

Sheila has been the mainstay of making all these arrangements. I don't know how we would have coped if she hadn't found the time and skills to engineer so many things.

When we moved Maggie out of the sub-acute rehab facility to Jody's house, we also enrolled her in hospice. Typically, this is done when the person is not expected to live more than six months. The medical perspective on this is that the caregivers and family accept that the patient will not survive the illness, and it is unlikely that she will improve at all. They move from a treatment goal of cure to one of providing comfort measures. This change sounds simple, and it's easily completed, but it has several implications.

Enrollment into hospice brings with it prompt access to various types of durable medical goods, like a hospital bed, portable suction, oxygen if needed, and the regular participation in care by hospice nurses. It also means that the physician who works for hospice will assume medical management, taking over for the previous physician. And, if the patient has been receiving physical therapy or speech therapy, it will cease. We tried to balance all of these options and then made our decision. We didn't ask Dad to play a significant role in this choice since our decision was largely based on the care provisions for equipment.

Jody's place has been the ultimate resting place for everybody. He has a beautiful home, built in the style of a Cotswold cottage, right on the Detroit River. He has arranged for the folks to live in the sunroom, a light and airy space with leaded glass windows and wood paneling. The art on the walls includes prints by Rembrandt and Picasso. To the east, one looks directly at the river with the occasional freighter going by; to the south is a view of manicured formal gardens.

The caregivers have settled right in, too. When I was there on an afternoon a few days ago, I watched one of them pull up a chair in the dining nook and sit down with a huge snack. There are two caregivers since there are several situations in which Maggie needs two people to help her move, and they need to relieve one another in order to provide 24-hour care.

The folks will move into a new place on October 2. This will be a rental home on the south end of the island, also looking out on the river. In this case, the view is to the west, toward Calf Island and the Humbug Nature Reserve. It's idyllic and soothing.

Last weekend, we learned that we have an offer on the house they bought in Crystal River, Florida. The good news is that the offer is exactly what Dad paid for the place in January. The bad news is that moving expenses, the real estate agent commission, repairs to make the house ready for sale, and the air ambulance to get them back to Detroit all added up to a pretty penny, and we aren't close to a break-even point on the deal. Nonetheless, we all breathed a great sigh of relief since the cash reserves to support Mom and Dad are running close to empty.

Maggie is at a stage now where she sleeps most of the day. Because of her contractures, she hasn't moved unassisted since her fall and leg fracture in January. When I got to the sunroom on a recent visit, Dad was resting in a reclining chair. Maggie was sleeping, but my first reaction was one of dismay. Even though I had just seen her a couple days before, she seemed to have lost a significant amount of weight. Her arms were so thin and wrapped completely in a white linen, to protect her fragile skin. She slept with her mouth half open. Her breathing pattern was regular but shallow.

I couldn't help myself in feeling for the first time that Maggie's end is near. Jody doesn't feel this is the case, and I respect his perspective since he is there with her every day. Most of all, Dad doesn't see it. As we sat there Friday, I commented on how much weight Maggie has lost. He felt it was just because the caregivers weren't feeding her enough. He also observed that they weren't helping her stand or do exercises. I answered that Maggie can't stand and that she hasn't done so in months. I offered my opinion that she was "just winding down." She's probably too weak to eat and has little will to do so. He replied, "Well, we just need to reverse that trend," he said brusquely. This was a poignant turn to their long love affair. I'm sure he means well, but I don't think he grasps the full picture.

On Monday, I was doing a little work in Jody's greenhouse. As dusk was settling in, I saw a deer saunter onto the property from the south side. He was a young buck with a modest set of antlers. I yelled at him to get him to leave, but he just ignored me. He strolled about a bit, and when I came out again, I saw him lounging on the front lawn. I presume he was just waiting for it to be a little darker before beginning the evening meal in one of Jody's gardens. Everyone loves the place!

— Felix

NOVEMBER 9, 2013

Dear Family,

Several weeks have passed since I wrote last. Maggie and Dad are settled in at their new place on South Pointe Drive. It's a lovely, large home. The lot also is large, maybe three or four acres, and it has about 150 feet of waterfront, with a dock in front. The house is spacious, with four bedrooms and picture windows providing sweeping views of the Detroit River.

Maggie is continuing noticeably in her gradual decline. Today, the three caregivers each reported her speaking a single word. Since I heard her say "fine" last week, that means there's been reports of four words since September 1. We have hired two full-time caregivers, with some part-time help, anticipating that Maggie needed two of them to move her from bed to chair and back. However, Maggie is now confined to her bed. The women turn her at regular intervals, left or right, but she has not been out of bed at all. They are very kind and gentle with her.

I think Dad is bored. We have tried our best to find activities for him, but he really has never enjoyed reading novels or watching television. He sits next to Maggie, who may open her eyes and look about intently, but most often, she is sleeping. He has his chair positioned so he can look out at the river. In the last couple days, he has taken to turning the TV on without the volume on (just to watch, in case something interesting comes on), and today he started reading some western pulp fiction by Louis L'Amour. He's on page 20 of the large-print edition.

Unfortunately, he's starting to slip in his cognitive skills. Most days he repeats a story he has told me that day or on my previous visit. Sometimes it's a trivial detail; other times it's a matter of considerable importance to him, like relating when he observed that Maggie had suddenly lost her speech function, which he interpreted as evidence of a small stoke. I wish I knew if these changes could just be attributed to the lack of stimulation and sensory deprivation, or to real cognitive decline.

There is a growing body of literature about the consequence of critical illness in leading to cognitive decline.[46] For patients with a serious illness that includes a serious infection (such as sepsis), which leads to delirium, the magnitude of the decrease in mental capacity is equivalent to minor brain trauma or to moderate Alzheimer's disease.

Dad has had enough medical problems over the past year to qualify for this. He had delirium after his back surgery one year ago, and I am told that he had periods of disorientation after he fractured his pelvis this spring. However, it may also just be the progression of the years, as he is now 93 years old.

On my previous visit, Dad asked an interesting question. He said, "I don't know what the purpose is for people to live so long, but I have decided that it's to increase the love. I don't know if that's really the purpose, but when you look at Sheila (i.e., Maggie), you can see how all the love is focused on her."

— Felix

DECEMBER 8, 2013

Dear Family,

We nearly got the whole family together for Thanksgiving Day. But, it was just impossible to coordinate the schedules of three families including the naptime of two infants. And, the house the folks rent just doesn't have the capability to host more than a few people for dinner. Jody and Sheila and their families stopped by Thursday. Sheila's son Chris took some traffic-stopping cute pictures of his wife, Vivien, and their son Elijah, which appear in the photo album.

Caroline and I went down to Grosse Ile on Saturday afternoon, and met our daughter Beth, her husband, Jim, and their son Teddy. We had a few snacks, and Teddy ran around for a while. Jim and Teddy sang a couple songs for Maggie, which I couldn't quite capture on film. Jim is an Episcopal priest, and he offered a prayer and blessing for Maggie, and her face seemed to indicate an appreciation for it. Teddy reserved his analysis for the end of the visit: "Granny, P-Pop (great-grandfather), old."

Then our family drove to one of my brother-in-law Frank's old haunts, the Auburn Cafe, a Greek restaurant set in the middle of a desolate stretch of suburban Detroit decay. We were the last to arrive and sat down to a long table of 20 or so family members. Jody and Rosemary were there with their daughters, Lindsey and Rachel, and Rachel's boyfriend Bob. Sheila and Frank were there with their kids, Chris and Rose, their spouses Vivien and Andreas, and their grandson Elijah.

The restaurant wasn't full yet since we had set an early dinner time, but the place was filled with the noisy chatter and laughter of our group.

Caroline sat down, looked around, and said, "This is a dream come true … to sit with so many family members in a boisterous and happy group." I don't know if it appeared to others to be a scene from the movie "My Big Fat Greek Wedding," but we were a happy group, three generations laughing and reconnecting over good times.

Fast forward to New York City, one weekend later. Alison needed a surgery for a skin cancer, and her husband, Randy, was out of town. We used this as a reason for Caroline to fly to New York to help Alison with baby Jack, and I took the opportunity to fly in Friday. I arranged for tickets so we could all go to the Frick museum to see the visiting collection from the Mauritshuis in the Hague, Netherlands.[47]

Home to the very best in Dutch Golden Age painting, the museum loaned out works as it undergoes renovation. The centerpiece of the Frick exhibit is Johannes Vermeer's "Girl With a Pearl Earring," one of the most famous paintings in the world. A single gallery was devoted to the Vermeer, and another 14 works were displayed in the East Gallery. The paintings are all from the time of the Dutch Old Masters and include several by Rembrandt. They touched on two themes popular in Holland at the time: morality and "tronies," a stylized painting, where the subject is given some exotic head dress.

Examples include Rembrandt's "Tronie" of a Man with a Feathered Beret (featuring a man wearing an outrageous black beret) and Vermeer's "Girl With a Pearl Earring" (depicting a young girl wearing a turban-like headscarf and pearl earring).

Likewise, the pearl in the painting's centerpiece is a fanciful addition. It's unlikely that pearls would ever be of such size, but they were sometimes used as symbols of chastity. Much of the enigmatic character of this painting comes from the juxtaposition of the girl's exotic head dress, the outsized pearl and her innocent face.

Most of the other works touched on the morality of the ideal household. The painting of Dutch interior scenes was staged to demonstrate the virtues of order, thrift and fidelity.

The exception to the staid and quietly moralistic paintings was the large painting that occupied the entire east wall of the gallery, "As the Old Sing, So Pipe the Young," by Jan Steen (whose name I learned is pronounced "stain"). This work captures three generations gathered to celebrate a baptism. It's filled with movement, clever details and audacious good humor. Besides his work as a premier artist of his time, Steen ran an inn, which apparently gave him plenty of source material for this work.

Toward the right in the painting, we see Steen himself with a huge smile, teaching his son to smoke. In the center is the confused family dog, and on the left, a woman with a partially opened blouse, warming her feet on a small furnace as she gets a glassful of wine. In the upper left, a parrot stands quietly, as a reminder that people will repeat what they hear and see, and our children will learn more from our actions than from pious instructions.

We weren't able to get four generations for our dinner, and if we had, it would have been subdued, in deference to the oldest ones. Our gathering of three generations might have come closer to that presented by Steen if we hadn't been cramped by travel schedules, the need for sleep training for the youngest and the impromptu nature of our evening.

The Frick exhibit of paintings was carefully put together. Of some 800 works at the Mauritshuis, these 15 were selected for the exhibit at the Frick. Imagine the decision-making in choosing just 15 works to cover representative painters, themes and styles. The resultant exhibit teaches a great life lesson. Our family has always been biased toward the idea of the virtuous life. I think Steen also gets it right: It's the life of the family, not some creed or belief system that really matters. And it gets at the heart of the matter: Would we rather talk about life or just go out and experience it to the fullest?

— Felix

DECEMBER 15, 2013

Dear Family,

I make a deliberate effort not to ascribe to negative statements about the weather, especially in the winter. I keep a few quips on hand such as, "There is no such thing as bad weather, just a bad choice in clothing," and "The best thing about Michigan is that you don't have to wait for good weather to do things outside."

Today, all of my best lines were tested.

I need to begin by mentioning that Caroline is in Washington, D.C., with her parents, so when I got home from work Friday, I went straight to work putting up the Christmas lights in the shrubs in front of the house, despite the cold virus that I had brewing. It's always a lackluster effort, and this year it was made more frustrating by not testing the bulbs before I put them up, as most of the lights were out. After replacing the bad bulbs, I managed to put a whole series of lights on the shrubs with the plug at the wrong end of the string, so I had to do it over again.

My cold was in full swing yesterday, but I hoped a good night's sleep would remedy that. It did help, and I was measurably better as I headed to work today. Then the challenge began. The first phone call was from Caroline. Just as a cab was scheduled to arrive and take her to the airport, her mother said that she was so weak she couldn't get out of bed. They had to cancel the cab and call an ambulance instead.

The next phone call was from one of the caregivers for Maggie and Dad. We've had a big snowfall here in Detroit, and the folks were snowed in. The weekend helper needed to get out, and her replacement needed to get in. Being on call at the hospital, I was tied up for a while. Lisa was in Phoenix, Jody was in New York, and Sheila (who has the most contacts for this sort of thing) was in Cologne, Germany. I sent a few text messages and emails. Jody had a name to call, which didn't work out, but he gave me a backup name if I could track the guy down.

I drove to the folks' home, where the wind was blowing snow across the yard and depositing it in swirling drifts over the driveway. One of the caregivers had parked her car directly in front of the driveway. I parked right behind her. I had heavy boots in the car, so I put them on and tightened my winter coat. The snowdrifts came up over the tops of my boots, and the wind whipped stinging crystals of snow against my face. When I came out of the house 10 minutes later, my footprints were already completely covered by the drifting snow.

Inside it was warm and cozy. Maggie was sleeping when I arrived, but she woke up and smiled. Maybe she saw me tracking snow in on my corduroy pants and was glad it wasn't her problem. Dad was at the lunch table, wearing about two weeks' worth of a rangy beard. The caregivers were cheerful, despite being at a loss about what to do next. They expected me to solve the problem.

Caroline called with an update on her mother's status. It looked as if she would be released without the diagnosis of a major problem. A truck with a huge plow on the front was blasting through a neighbor's driveway, but I didn't get out in time, and he sped down the street to his next scheduled stop. As I left to continue my rounds at the hospital, I saw three young men pull up, snow shovels in hand. I offered them $30 in advance to clear the folks' driveway, which they readily accepted. Later I learned that they only cleared a path as wide as a sidewalk and then moved on, cash in hand. The good news is that the caregiver Nela later hailed a neighbor with a snow blower, who came to the rescue.

I drove down South Pointe Drive and turned onto West River Road, heading in the direction of our old childhood home. To the left, the river was angry gray and choppy, splashing icy water onto the shore. The wind had whipped streaks of snow across the road, not yet big enough to form drifts. The locust trees had dark trunks, and their branches twisted with dynamic asymmetry, as if made for the wind in winter.

I was driving Caroline's car, which was warm and quiet. On the radio, a Vivaldi oboe concerto filled the space with sound.

— Felix

JANUARY 20, 2014

Dear Family,

Things have been solid with Maggie and Dad, but I had a sudden event, which lasted just 10 seconds, and had a powerful impact.

Life has been a generally quiet routine for the ancient ones. For weeks now, the folks have been on a pleasant course. The caregivers are very sweet and genuinely considerate. Maggie and Dad have been healthy and appear to be happy. It's been great having all four of us kids in the vicinity for much of the last month, including the holidays. While Sheila and Jody have both been out of town a bit, Lisa and I have been able to visit more during those times. I think we made the most of the holiday celebrations.

The sudden event occurred at work a couple weeks ago. I was at the front desk, checking a patient out, when I overheard my receptionist tell a caller, "He is here. In fact, he just walked up. I'll put him on."

She placed the phone on hold and told me it was the Grosse Ile police wanting to talk with me. I waved that I would take it in a more private location, and she added with concern, "I hope everything is OK."

As I walked back to my work area, my mind raced to the consideration that this might be the phone call I have been anticipating and dreading for a few years now. It wasn't until I picked up the handset that I experienced a deep, descending, hollow, awful pain. I couldn't localize it, but it seemed central. It just lasted a few seconds, and I was aware that I had never felt anything like this before. The voice on the other end got to the point immediately, "This is the police, and we are calling about a death."

Of course, since the folks were fine on this day that I am writing, you, the reader, know that it had to be about the death of one of my patients. It was a young man who had been a patient in the practice nearly 30 years and who was found at home by his brother.

We try to be consistent in writing letters of condolence to the family after one of our patients has died. I'll need to write a letter to this person's family. We usually have several letters each month. (It's the nature of my practice — I'm not a bad doctor!). At times, these notes feel like a burden, and it's tempting to use pat phrases or say the same thing to each family. One thing I've avoided, especially for longtime patients, is to reassure the members of the patient's family that I know no matter how long they have tried to prepare themselves for the death of their family member, they can never be fully prepared for the event when it arrives. I think I did write this at some point, until it occurred to me that the grief response is so complicated that I was just being glib in making such a statement, so I stopped.

I recall a conversation I had at least 20 years ago with the conductor of the Pittsburgh Symphony Chorus. Caroline and I had just attended a live performance of the Mozart Requiem that he conducted. He asked for my reactions to the music, not for the performance itself. I told him I was at a loss for several of the sections, since I hadn't ever experienced emotions like those that Mozart was expressing, for example, the Rex tremendae majestatis (Mighty King) or the Dies irae (Day of Judgment). I just couldn't relate to rage like that. The conductor was quizzical but polite.

It's daunting to think that our bodies harbor the potential to produce all kinds of sensations that we have never experienced, but which may, in fact, lie in our future. For example, I've never passed a kidney stone, but I know enough people who have. It's a marvel of our creation that I have a set of pain fibers in my ureters, which have been on standby for more than 60 years, ready to send the "warning" that I am about to pass a stone. I'd just as soon have them never get the chance to flex their neurons.

What was that strange and distasteful sensation I had when I picked up the phone? It's hard to offer a biologic explanation, such as, "That was just activation of a set of nerves that also help you know a certain food is bad for you." I've had plenty of bad food in my day and enough different specific and nonspecific stimuli to know this is nothing like anything I've ever experienced before.

Now I'm back to waiting again for that phone call about my parents. I've had a foretaste of what my reaction will be. With respect to the Mozart Requiem, I have at least known some people who have had the types of emotion that Mozart expresses in it, and I've seen such emotion in art or drama, so I'm getting closer. Our family and friends, our local community of concern, act like a nerve net in interpreting the events they experience to prepare the rest of us for what lies ahead. In this regard, it's a blessing that I have my immediate family and then our extended family to call upon.

— Felix

JULY 17, 2014

Dear Family,

We helped Maggie celebrate her 96th birthday today. Lisa arranged for helium balloons, and the caregivers prepared a birthday party with cake and ice cream, and fresh strawberries and blueberries. Nela had a patio rose that was just starting to open. Tea was served at 4:30 p.m.

Sheila and Frank brought several gifts, including some CDs that Maggie will enjoy and a unique animal (either a giraffe or a llama) made of a metal frame covered with moss, with cactus and succulents growing on it to form the skin and body parts like the tail. Sheila Shelton was the special guest, bringing flowers wrapped in purple tissue, the same color as her blouse.

Our delightful caregivers had placed a new set of pink sheets on the bed and dressed Maggie in a new matching pink sleep gown. For her part, when I arrived Maggie had just finished her afternoon smoothie, a homemade drink of pureed strawberries and blueberries. She seemed to appreciate the special attention. I gave Maggie a birthday card from all of us in my immediate family, a card based on the Vincent Van Gogh painting of sunflowers. It took several minutes of coaching to get her to open the card, and she stared at it a long time before it ended up on her lap, upside down, as the guests were arriving for the party.

Maggie was nonverbal the whole time I was there, neither speaking nor nodding her head in response to our comments or questions to her. I asked Nela how long it had been since she had heard Maggie say any words at all. She guessed about two months, which matches my estimate.

My sister Sheila told an endearing story about Stephanie, who was described in these Maggie Letters two years ago as the primary caregiver. She has been invited back not as a caretaker, but just to spend some time with the folks. Sheila gave Stephanie some background about the parents in their roles as physicians, as a way to try to establish a context in which Maggie might be engaged in conversation. She said that as a doctor, Dad provided the "intellect" and Maggie provided the "heart." Following up on that, Stephanie asked Maggie what kind of a doctor she was. It took a while to get her to say something, and then Maggie answered, "a good one."

Maybe I'm reading too much into this brief reply, but I was greatly encouraged by this short answer. It indicated that she is following our conversations, even though she seems detached. And she can connect the dots and make a coherent response. Most importantly, I was impressed with the good humor and confidence contained in that response. Our father is nationally famous for his clinical expertise, but Maggie never was one to slink in his shadow.

— Felix

AUGUST 17, 2014

Dear Family,

It seems like I'm in a dry spell in terms of these Maggie Letters. The irony is that my emotional life is on overload, while the state of my parents' lives seems relatively bland. It may also be that the saga has continued so long that it has the aspects of "a sad story with an unhappy ending," to borrow a phrase I heard in church today.

Maybe it will help to share a perspective on things from another event. Yesterday, I went to the memorial service for Greg Jones, one of my high school classmates, and for his mother, Shirley. From the get-go, it seemed like an odd situation. Greg never married, and his father died early on, after accumulating three yachts and a couple of motorcycles. Greg moved in with his mother soon after that. His mother died at age 90 in late June of this year; Greg died a month later.

The service was held in the chapel at St. James Church on Grosse Ile, where I first attended church more than 60 years ago. Just sitting there brought back a flood of memories, which were intensified when a couple of high school classmates joined me in the pew.

The service was poignant because of the folksy presentation by the minister, the Rev. Phil Dinwiddy, who asked for participation from the people present. The Jones' dog, Fido, was there, and he was called to the front at one point. I was impressed that people spoke of common things and recollected benign events, like things the Jones' dog had done. I was reminded that funerals can bring out simple acts that touch our hearts, as opposed to heroic events. Greg's life had proven him to be a brilliant thinker, and a calm and methodical lawyer who was beloved by his professional colleagues. He didn't have much extended family.

A man in the back spoke up. I don't know his name, but I think he is a local actor on the island who attends the church. He asked an interesting question. When we die, who will be there to speak up for us? He linked that to Greg's career as a lawyer, since our tradition in the United States calls for everyone to have counsel, no matter what their income level. I stayed with the idea of people speaking up at the time of our death. Apart from an uncle of Greg's who came in from the east coast, there were no family members.

Grief is such a complex emotion. The accepted reason to attend a funeral may be to offer support and consolation to the grieving family. But today, with almost no family present, our speaker raised the concern of needing to speak for the deceased. Why would we need anyone to speak up for us, as if we needed to justify or defend our life? My own thoughts were far away. The service and the contemplation on the life of Greg and his mother was a deep consolation for me, even with no family there.

At the reception that followed, I spoke with several people whom I hadn't known, but who knew of our family over the years. Some asked me to be remembered to my parents. One woman my age thanked me for the care that I had given her husband, an anesthesiologist, who died 18 months ago. She bounced back from that to run the Boston Marathon in 2013, but she didn't complete it because of the terrorist attack bombings at the finish line. She did finish it this year. She's been working out with weights, and she flashed her bare leg out at me, and I was obligated to admire her well-muscled gams.

From the funeral service, I went to see Maggie and Dad. Both were asleep and didn't wake up despite my calls to them or jostling from the Polish caregivers. Dad had a stroke on August 5, which affected his speech and ability to swallow. The speech improved, but he never regained his ability to swallow. He had a feeding tube placed in his stomach on August 11 and went home the next day. Last night he had been up every 20 minutes with abdominal discomfort, which prevented him and the caregivers from getting any sleep.

It turns out that he also had disturbed Maggie's sleep. When he rings the bell for assistance, Maggie hears it, two rooms away from where Dad sleeps. The caregiver verified this, asking her if she wakes up with the bell and noting that Maggie nodded her head yes. Mom and Dad have been married over 70 years, and she maintains concern for his well-being.

Here's a paradoxical aspect of a sad story with an unhappy ending: We tend to magnify our own grief when we are in touch with everyone else's grief. At the same time, when we share our feelings, it has a remarkable ability to attenuate sadness and suffering. Maybe that explains our lighthearted comments at the funeral. In this case, we weren't in the position of offering solace to the family, but instead taking a warm and forgiving look at the mother and son who died within a month of one another, finding in that a love story of an entirely different character.

— Felix

AUGUST 31, 2014

Dear Family,

I awoke yesterday feeling dull. Moreover, I was stiff and sore as well. There it was, the day before my father was to turn 94 years old, and I was the one leading the chorus of complaints about the challenges of aging.

Dull may be the most insidious negative emotion. It so easily sneaks up on us, like that fog with little cat feet, I guess. It also reminds me of the diary entries by the ancestor many of us share, A.B. McGown, writing about his long nautical journey to South America. For several consecutive days, the apparent sameness and boredom of travel near the equator led him to post identical entries:

> "*8 a.m. Turned out.*
> *10 p.m. Turned in.*"

I've felt that way so often on my visits to see Maggie and Dad. It's hard to believe that next month marks the one-year anniversary of Maggie's enrollment into hospice. Normally, a person isn't eligible for hospice unless the life expectancy is less than six months. We've had to renew her enrollment twice. Since nothing seemed to have changed when this most recent renewal came up, it was a challenge to determine if Maggie would qualify again. She made it, because the hospice nurse measured the circumference of her arm, and it showed continued volume loss. I noticed a more diffuse change when I bent over to kiss Maggie goodbye yesterday, and my hands felt her hips and shoulders, which were so tiny, so frail and so bony.

Each visit is very much the same. Maggie is either asleep, or she lies quietly, staring ahead. When she is awake, she holds her mouth in a firm half-smile. When she is asleep, she looks terrible. If the ultimate expression of cuteness is "sleeping like a baby," there is a direct opposite, and that is the unguarded sleep of an old person, mouth open with an ungainly expression and, possibly, the eyes half-open as well.

Dad did have something to celebrate on his birthday. He has been working with the speech therapist on swallowing. To retrain his swallow mechanism, he is taught to avoid the prototypical swallow, where we toss our head back to down a few vitamins or chug a beer, but instead to tip the chin onto the chest and then swallow. This is counterintuitive, but it has helped. He was able to eat a small bowl of soup yesterday.

All of us make a strong effort to prevent boredom and dullness for our parents. Sheila is able to visit every day, and Jody and I try to get there several times a week. Whenever Lisa can get up from Cleveland, it's a real treat, especially since she brings Bentley, who shows natural talent as a therapy dog. Still, the situation is daunting, when there are no other visitors besides us, and Dad spends the entire day sitting with Maggie, who is unable to communicate in any meaningful manner.

I was able to shake my dullness Saturday by listening to a guided meditation on mindfulness. My daily reading on Sunday[48] had given me the word to examine this process: "apatheia," a term used by the early desert fathers before Christianity became a religion. We might tend to translate this as "apathy." Wikipedia suggests "equanimity" rather than "indifference." In the tradition of mindfulness meditation, we are encouraged to be alert to the things around us, without getting caught up in a story or narrative about them. That story often leads to daydreaming, and before we know it, we have lost our chance to be present in the moment. Being "indifferent" to the sights and sounds around us is, paradoxically, a way to be alert and fresh.

Given the course life takes, it's inevitable that things will become stale again, and I'm grateful that there are effective weapons against dullness. After all, with enough effort, dullness does evaporate like the fog.

— Felix

SEPTEMBER 17, 2014

Dear Family,

I stopped to see Maggie yesterday. Usually I wait until the afternoon because Dad doesn't get up until the crack of noon or later. However, we've been concerned about Maggie for the past 24 hours since she has developed a deep, rasping cough. The last thing a person in her condition needs is a bit of pneumonia. Jody had phoned in a prescription for her the day before.

It was a beautiful, sunny day when I crossed the bridge to Grosse Ile, with cool temperatures and fluffy white clouds. The water had the glassy calm that reflected the trees and the sky. They had to move from the rental home on short notice and are now in a new condominium complex that is directly next door to where I grew up. At the condo, the birds have discovered the bird feeder. Debris was everywhere from earlier visitors to the feeder that had tossed a lot of seeds as they ate with abandon. Now birds covered the little balcony.

Maggie was lying on her left side, and I sat down so we could be face to face. She seemed comfortable. At times, she coughed with a deep, rattling sound. She didn't seem to have a fever. Our eyes met, and I began to talk. I always assume that she can hear me and understand what I am saying.

I told her about the last few weeks: our trip to Baltimore to see Beth and Jim, and their son Teddy, our trip to Lansing over the past weekend to help Alison continue to move into her new home and Caroline's trip to northern Virginia. She had flown out to visit her mother, who had a stroke while Caroline was there. So she had to extend her visit in order to get her mother to the emergency room and then to an outpatient visit with a neurologist.

I peered into Maggie's face and eyes, trying to discern if she understood what I was saying. She just lay there on her side, breathing quietly. So, I went ahead and told her about the news I had gotten just last week. Her nephew Gus McGown, the son of her brother Cameron, had died of cancer last week. He was 65 years old.

Maggie seemed to listen intently. I felt more certain that she was listening because she maintained my gaze the entire time I was talking. When I finished, she let her eyes close partway. Her hands still tapped out the rhythm that she has repeated for at least three years now. Then she closed her eyes all the way, took a deep, relaxed sigh and stopped the tapping. I just sat there with her for a few silent minutes. It was very quiet and peaceful. The birds fluttered on the balcony, and the breeze through the open doorway was cool.

I kissed Maggie goodbye and got up to go to the office. I reflected that one day I would hold my last conversation with this dear, grand lady. At that time, this would be a special day to remember.

I wasn't far into the day's work this morning when Sheila called to tell me that Maggie's breathing pattern was worse, and she seemed to be struggling a bit. Sheila made a ton of phone calls to try to find the best care environment to get a chest X-ray and some blood work done, but they ended up in the hospital emergency room. The physicians and staff were great, and Maggie got attentive care. The X-ray was reported as normal, but the ER physician was concerned, on clinical grounds, that she had pneumonia. She administered two powerful antibiotics by IV, and the doctor then arranged for them to be given at home in liquid form. Maggie returned home a couple of hours later, and Sheila sent me a text about how glad Dad was to see her back home.

It's now been just over a year since Maggie was enrolled in hospice care. The hospice nurse stopped by and spent a lot of time at the bedside. She was very helpful. Even if we buy a good deal of time with these antibiotics, there's no escaping the fact that Maggie is nearing the end of her remarkable journey. I can't help but notice that she is doing so with dignity and grace, despite her nonverbal status. And, I am so grateful that I have the support of my three siblings, and the love and concern of our wider family as we enter this phase.

— Felix

P.S. My cousin Dirk sent a picture of his brother Gus and this short note:

"To lose a sibling is one [thing] that only when it happens to you can you understand others' loss. I was told we are starting to regain some of our lives when we don't wake up thinking of our loss, as our first conscious thought.

"Gus loved a 'battle' as you probably understood from the newspaper article that accompanied this note.

I was amused when talking with his children that they hadn't heard, that in his more rebellious youth, he had a mild confrontation with the Rolling Stones when they came to Sydney.

"Shauna had Gus buried in a nostalgic country cemetery near their local town called Bollon in Queensland. It is a quiet, dusty resting place by a billabong with a majestic gum tree. Tourists, who we call "grey nomads," pull up by the banks in their four-wheel drives and vans to take in the tranquility. Gus loved bottle trees, and I was taken that there is one directly between his grave and the billabong, what some locals call the lagoon when it is full."

Gus McGown, photo for his obituary, 2014

SEPTEMBER 25, 2014

Dear Family,

In my experience, when one makes a reference to a sister, it may be an excuse for an insult or derogatory comment. For years, here in Detroit, our most popular newspaper columnist, Jim Fitzgerald, often referred to his wife's sister as the source of all sorts of sinister ideas and reprehensible activities. Only later did we learn that his wife never did have a sister.

In a similar vein, this week, one of my most colorful patients, Dick Whitwam, came by the office, and he did Jim Fitzgerald one better. He bragged about his dog and complained about his wife's sister. I don't remember what he said about his "sister-in-law," but I do remember what he said about his dog. He said that his dog only had two legs, "and he wasn't very fast, since both legs were on the same side." His wife added that she never had a sister, and Dick never had a dog.

In this case, I do have a sister. In fact, I have two of them. Although they are both remarkable, I want to comment on Sheila since she fits into the events of the last few days. In my last post, I spoke about the trip to the emergency department at the hospital. Sheila handled all of the arrangements to get Maggie picked up by ambulance and get her to the ER. I met them there.

I left an important event out of that post. When Maggie returned from X-rays to her area, Cart Number 9 in the Emergency Department, she became apprehensive, as if she were having a panic attack. Her heart rate increased and her blood pressure shot up to about 180/112. I did my best to reassure the nurses, Sheila and caregiver Nela that the high blood pressure was not serious but instead just represented a response to Maggie's anxiety, which was likely triggered by the strange setting and the many people she saw on the trip to the X-ray Department and back.

This is so typical of the world of medicine: While I was in this professional mode, and busy looking smart for the ER staff and Nela, Sheila was actually attending to Maggie, calming her down with soothing phrases and words of reassurance. In just a few minutes, Maggie's breathing pattern slowed down, her heart rate decreased and her blood pressure returned to the normal range.

I do intend for these Maggie Letters to include an aspect of a practical manual for the understanding and care of people with Alzheimer's disease, so I should add another note about Maggie's condition the day after her trip to the hospital. While it is true that she seemed to be much better the next day, she, of course, still had attributes of advanced dementia. She continued her tap, tap, tapping motions with her hands. However, she also continued something she had started in the ER. She was grinding her teeth so forcefully that I could hear her doing so across the room. Even though she was back at the condo and out of the stressful ER setting, she continued this grinding. Part of the reason I am unable to understand her limited speech is that she is now missing several of her bottom incisors. Nela told me that she had scooped a tooth out of Maggie's mouth earlier today.

Now, these are 96-year-old teeth, and it used to be commonplace for people that age to have had all their teeth replaced, but I think it is worth a pause to consider the implications of grinding teeth so intensely they begin to shed. I don't think there is anything we can do about this since she is beyond reasoning. It was reassuring that she was no longer grinding the next day when I visited.

Since Maggie seems to be recovering from this respiratory infection, I want to reflect on this long journey of hers. If there are families looking at a parent or loved one with Alzheimer's disease, it's reasonable to look at the situation from a long-term care perspective. And, I want to keep the role of my sister at the forefront.

First of all, providing such care is exhausting, taking quite a toll, both physically and mentally. Initially, uncertainty dominates when these things are new to all of us. Later, the need to establish care and support becomes the dominant feature, as the person declines so much that family alone — especially the spouse — is unable to provide the needed care on his/her own. Later still, this care becomes progressively more specialized and expensive. At our present stage, we need two 24-hour caregivers who keep up the house, shop and provide all the meals, as well as tend to every personal need. In addition, we have a parade of other specialized people who come into the home: a massage therapist and the hospice nurse for Maggie, and a physical therapist for Dad.

Sheila has organized all of the details related to each one of these items, while Frank took on the role of manager of all the finances. And then there is meal planning, shopping list preparation and organization of all the schedules. On top of that, Sheila carves out time from her schedule to visit every day.

Now here's an interjection from my early memories of Maggie. She certainly was the "captain of the ship" when we kids were all in school. For some of that time, she also ran a medical practice. Talk about skills in multi-tasking! She made sure all of us had some time together as a family before we headed off to school. I think it's fair to say there were moral underpinnings to her instruction.

Somehow, I drew the conclusion that the purpose of our instruction at home, school and church was to learn to be a better person. Years later, I read "A Path with Heart,"[47] a life-changing book for me, which gave me a jolt: The real purpose of our life journey is to see the world with a heart of kindness. In the years since then, I've found that the proper measuring stick of my progress is how much I am growing in love and happiness. All of the rest — financial return, professional advancement, intellectual achievement — is secondary.

If the proof of the pudding is in the tasting, the test of this rule is in our later years. When we survey the world of Alzheimer's disease and the effect it has on the family, it's fair to ask how we measure up. The measuring stick we use can't be based on the expense of daily care, the employment of professional caregivers or other such metrics. I think the only mark is seeing the world with a heart of kindness and growing in love and happiness.

At this stage, nothing else we can do will have significant impact on Maggie and Dad, although I don't want to minimize the benefit of the care we provide. I'm especially grateful that Sheila is leading the way in this regard. All of us appreciate the one who leads all of us with a heart of kindness.

— Felix

OCTOBER 20, 2014

Dear Family,

Last weekend, Caroline and I went up to our place in Canada to close it down for the season. It was a trip filled with nostalgic memories since we drove up with our best friends from the Detroit area. The trees in northern Ontario, known for the fabulous color change in the fall, were at their peak. It is said that the colors are most vibrant when the leaves are wet. It rained just about continuously when we were there, and I craved the chance to see if a little sunshine would have made a difference.

On the way up, we remembered several trips that we took with Maggie five or 10 years ago, when she was in the early to middle stages of her decline into Alzheimer's disease. One time we got an hour or so north of Detroit, and she got worried that we were lost. "Joe, do you think Felix knows where we are?" and, "How will we find our way back from here?" Dad was calm and soothing as he spoke gently with Maggie and reassured her that we knew exactly where we were and would have no trouble getting home again.

People with Alzheimer's disease are famous for wandering off and getting into unusual predicaments, or for just getting lost. We now have some clues from the world of neuroscience about this phenomenon. This year, the Nobel Prize in medicine went to three people who discovered the brain's "inner GPS," as it was called in the presentation.[50] The first insight came in 1971, when John O'Keefe discovered the inner navigational system in rats. He identified nerve cells in the hippocampus region of the brain that were always activated when a rat was in a certain location. He called these "place cells" and showed that rats built inner maps in different environments.

The second discovery came in 2005 when husband and wife team Edvard and May-Britt Moser found a component of the brain's positioning system by identifying other nerve cells that permit coordination and positioning, calling these "grid cells." While mapping connections to the hippocampus, they discovered a pattern of activity in the nearby entorhinal cortex. When a rat passed multiple locations, the cells formed a hexagonal grid. Together, the place and grid cells allowed the animals to determine position and to navigate.

Recent studies now show that place and grid cells exist in humans, as demonstrated in brain-imaging studies and from electrode stimulations during neurosurgery. This may lead to a better understanding of the events that lead to Alzheimer's disease, where the hippocampus and entorhinal cortex are often damaged in the early stages of the disease, with affected individuals losing their way and failing to recognize the environment.

"A Caregiver's Guide to Alzheimer's Disease" describes some of the problems of ambulation in patients with moderate-stage dementia. The authors advise to stick with familiar places when traveling. And to keep vacations simple and slow-paced, while considering taking several short trips rather than one long one.

It all makes sense in retrospect: I can see now how we bit off too long a travel segment when we left for Canada. The trip usually takes about seven hours. We typically stop halfway there, but that would have been in a location that was new, and also strange, to Maggie. Also, in retrospect, the fear and anxiety that I described in the last Maggie Letter about her trip to the ER may have been as much related to the change in place as it was to the unknown faces and medical procedures.

Nonetheless, on our trips Up North, Maggie never seemed to tire of pointing out trees and shrubs at their peak. The northern part of Michigan is all rolling hills covered with red maples and oaks, yellow-leaved birch and aspen, and deep green pines and hemlocks. It is a beautiful sight.

There are pictures that I took earlier this month and they are shown in the photo gallery, with the fond regret that I wish Maggie and Dad could have been with us.

— Felix

CHAPTER TEN

The Final Chapter

NOVEMBER 9, 2014

Dear Family,

Jody and I were in the office together on Tuesday. Our cell phones rang at the same time. Since he has a spiffy iPhone and I have this hapless Blackberry, my call went straight to voicemail, and I heard him pick up the line. Our caregiver Nela had called each of us because Maggie had just had a seizure. She called 911 before trying to get in touch with us, and the ambulance driver was there by the time she got Jody on the phone.

I listened as Nela reviewed what had happened: Maggie had been in her usual state of health when Nela observed her to turn to the right. Her eyes rolled back and then deviated to the right. She brought her hands up to her chest, and they began to shake. The episode lasted about two or three minutes, and then she seemed to collapse and was nonresponsive.

Nela put the ambulance driver on the phone. He had been correctly taught to check for neurologic changes following a grand mal seizure to determine whether a person has also had a stroke. The first thing to observe is that the seizure patient regains consciousness and then they regain speech facility, which may lag by several minutes (whereas a stroke patient may not speak at all). What I overheard made it clear that the driver was concerned about Maggie in this regard. I heard Jody say that Maggie hasn't said a word in months, and that this event doesn't call for her to go to the ER.

It was clear we had a conflict here, that Nela and the ambulance driver thought Maggie needed to be bundled up and transported to the hospital ASAP. Jody prevailed by telephone. He and I verified that we were in agreement on a few points related to health care directives. I left to go straight to the house, and Jody got on the phone to Sheila and Lisa to verify that the approach we recommended would be in agreement with their views. These things had been discussed last year, and I had overseen end-of-life healthcare directives for both Maggie and Dad. Of course, they have moved twice since then, and getting our hands on the papers would be no easy matter. More than that, it's one thing to make a decision about intensity of care when the person is perfectly stable and completely different when they have a sudden change in their condition.

Driving to the house, I crossed the bridge to Grosse Ile, which I have done thousands of times since I was 3 years old. It was dusk, and the water was glassy calm. Later, a nearly full moon would rise. This crossing, however, felt different, with an overlay of foreboding, and I couldn't stop myself from reviewing a few scenarios. We are taught to do this in medicine since it helps us be focused on the problem at hand when we arrive at the scene of a critically ill patient. Later, thinking back on this trip to my mother's side, I came up with the idea that family events like this are dress rehearsals for the actual moment when the person dies.

Maggie was noticeably upset, and she held her head rigidly, the way she had done when she was so frightened in the hospital ER a few weeks ago. I sat on the bed and held her thin, bony hand. She turned her head in my direction when I spoke to her. Nela reviewed the events and told me she was so distraught that she just called the ambulance immediately. I think the decision not to go to the hospital was the only logical one. After all, Maggie has been in hospice for a year now. While I was there, Dad asked several times if we should take Maggie to the hospital.

Lisa has told me that the most common cause of seizures in the elderly is a previous stroke. As I sat with Maggie, Dad expressed his concern. He wanted to know if Maggie was going to be all right and asked again if we should take her to the hospital. I said the event was over, Maggie was doing fine, and it was likely that it had occurred because she had a stroke sometime in the past. He then offered that he thought Maggie had had a stroke two years ago, before they moved to Florida. She had suddenly stopped talking and was unresponsive for a few minutes although she didn't fall to the floor. He hadn't taken her to the hospital then.

By the next day, it was clear that this was just one more event in Maggie's progressive downhill slide. The emails between Jody, Sheila,

Lisa and me were focused more on Dad's condition. He's not sleeping well. He seems to have a major degree of cognitive decline, but this has been difficult for us to assess, in part, because he is so hard of hearing, but also because he continues to be so evasive about his own health status.

All of us are concerned that his cognitive loss is related to significant sensory deprivation. He surely must be completely bored. He sleeps poorly at night, calling for the caregivers every hour or so to get up to go to the bathroom. He doesn't seem to be able to go, but then he is incontinent the next time they check on him. He sleeps until noon the next day. He spends the entire day at Maggie's side. Since she is completely nonverbal, there is no interaction, no conversation. He can't eat because of his stroke, and gets all meals by the feeding tube. He can drink a little, and he enjoys tiny amounts of ice cream on occasion.

We've tossed around ideas such as playing cards or board games, like checkers, or sitting with him to watch TV, commenting as the show goes on. He has never enjoyed any of such things, and he didn't seem to have much interest in them when I asked about them, assuming, that is, that he heard me.

On Friday, I took Caroline's car to work, since the seats are lower than in my SUV. When I got to the folks' house, Maggie seemed to be back to her usual state of health. I asked Dad if he wanted to take a ride in the car with me. Of course, I asked three times since he answered unrelated questions at first. It was a beautiful evening, with cobalt blue skies, a crisp chill in the air, and a few vibrant yellow and red leaves hanging on to the trees. We took a 30-minute spin around the island, driving by our childhood home and the location of the house he left two years ago. I think it must have been torn down about 10 minutes after he moved out, but the new owners have built a very attractive home on the site.

It really wasn't too much of a battle to get him in and out of the car, and it was clear we should have done this long before. Back at the house, the first order of business was a quick trip to the potty. He came out, not in the wheelchair that delivered him there, but pushing his walker and loudly singing a song he made up on the spot, a paraphrase of "Oh, what a beautiful morning."

— Felix

DECEMBER 1, 2014

Dear Family,

We celebrated Thanksgiving on Thursday with the closest thing to a complete Rogers Family reunion that we have seen in some time. There was plenty of the chaos that marks a memorable family get-together. We missed the members who could not be with us.

The grand vision was that all of us would contribute food for the meal, and we would all take the time to stop by the condo to see Maggie and Dad before dinner started promptly at 5 p.m. Caroline and I were the first to get to the folks, soon after 4. Jody and his boys arrived as we were leaving (see photo album). Lisa was delayed en route from Cleveland and got there a bit after 5. The positive spin on this was that it meant the others would be visiting in batches over the long weekend, so the folks would have plenty of company.

It was a tough visit with Maggie and Dad. Caroline and Alison hadn't seen Dad for a while, and it was a shock for them to see how much he has slipped. Dad had suffered a stroke a couple of months ago, and he was clearly subdued. In addition to the chronic problem of his poor hearing, his speech was slow, at times dissociated from the theme of the conversation, and his voice is so soft that it was hard to hear and understand him. We pulled chairs around the recliner chair where Dad spends his day and the hospital bed where Maggie now lives. We tried to get grandson Jack to visit with the folks, as Elijah did with such a photogenic flourish last year.

However, Jack is naturally shy, and he was in a strange environment. And he was fascinated by the toy house we had brought with us. He could activate a whole series of sounds and lights by pushing the right buttons. After a while, we got the idea to put this on Dad's lap, and Jack went over to play with the toy. Maggie seemed to be very aware of the presence of this little guy in the room and followed him with her eyes. She moved her hand out in his direction and began her tap, tap, tapping motion, this time in a continuous pattern. With a little persuasion, we pulled Jack in her direction and brought his hand up to hers. Bless his heart, he grabbed her hand and held it as he tried to keep playing with the house in Dad's lap. It didn't last long, but it was a precious moment.

Dinner was characteristically Rogerian, with a wide variety of food requirements, from vegan to gluten-free to food for infants. In addition,

we had everything blended to go through a feeding tube for Dad and into
a smoothie for Maggie. We had cocktails, wine and nonalcoholic fruit
and vegetable drinks. This was a far-ranging potluck, including both local
contributions and items from Chicago, Sheila's stepson Scooter's new
grocery and gourmet food business, and more varieties of potatoes than
you can imagine. (Longtime readers of these letters will want to know
that there were no rutabagas.)

It's hard to believe that these letters started four years ago this
month. They began as a series of emails designed to keep my siblings up
to date on an injury Maggie sustained when she fell. They then morphed
into an antemortem eulogy for Maggie and a personal exploration
of Alzheimer's disease. Now they are expanding to include Dad's
unfortunate decline into cognitive impairment.

Maggie has exhibited a remarkably long and inexorably slow
downhill journey. Of course, we really didn't know what to expect when
her illness first became manifest, and the books on the topic don't help
much. Even though she is deeply impaired, it is gratifying to see that
her few remaining mental functions are centered on relationships with
the family. She does appreciate our visits to her, and she follows the
conversations and those who come and go.

In contrast, Dad seems to be racing to catch up. Maybe his
pathophysiology is different, since we suspect that a stroke played a
major role in his deterioration. There are a variety of causes of dementia,
and they can follow widely different time courses. We are also concerned
that he is depressed. There are a lot of reasons for depression, including
his stroke, his social isolation and the impact of spending each day at the
bedside of Maggie, now his wife of 71 years, and watching her quietly slip
away from him.

Lisa and I talked about how best to keep Dad engaged and to slow the
progression of his impairment. It's one thing to read about activities that
can delay the onset or progression of dementia and another to be able to
implement those suggestions. For example, exercise is a proven modality,
but it's taking increasingly more effort for Dad to get out of his chair and
into the wheelchair. We used to insist that he walk to the bathroom, and
now he barely gets into the wheelchair. While social engagement has
been shown to be beneficial, it is hard to explain why it's so difficult to
communicate with Dad and engage him in conversation. It seems to be

more than just loss of hearing. It's hard to imagine bringing in an outsider at this stage given these difficulties in communication.

My next Maggie Letter will touch on the topic of normal and abnormal aging of the brain and revisit some of the issues on prevention of Alzheimer's disease.

— Felix

DECEMBER 6, 2014

Dear Family,

With Dad's descent into cognitive impairment, after so many years at the top of his game, I want to reassess our current understanding of the biology of the aging brain. Although we tend to focus on the negative side, like Alzheimer's disease, for example, there is a positive side, like the progression in wisdom that is part of the process of growth and maturation.

Most of the early studies on aging relied on natural history observations of defined populations that were followed for decades. Several of these are summarized in the current issue of *Science* magazine: [51]

In Sweden, more than 2,000 identical and nonidentical twins were followed to compare those who lived in separate homes from those who remained together to define the roles of genetics and environment.

The U.S. nun study used an archive of essays written when the women applied to the convent at age 22 as a marker of cognitive ability.

More than 900 centenarians in Okinawa, Japan, comprise a long-running study that examines genetic and lifestyle factors in the unusual longevity and lucidity in this cohort.

A decades-old study from Scotland is now using IQ tests to assess how the brain ages. By coincidence, a report in this same issue of *Science* magazine[52] highlights the story of one of those people, Sheila McGowan, who was 11 years old on June 4, 1947. (Our Sheila McGown, aka, Maggie, would have been 28 on that day.) On this date, in her hometown of Glasgow, this other Sheila McGowan joined more than 70,000 school children throughout Scotland as part of one of the first efforts to measure the intelligence of an age cohort across an entire nation. Sadly, the original goal of the surveys was to determine how many students were mentally defective and unlikely to benefit from schooling.

Science magazine followed Sheila after the exam: Her mother died the following April, and she lived alone with her father, who worked the night shift. She had scored high on the intelligence test, but like many other poor teenagers at the time, dropped out of school at age 16. Decades passed. She married and had two daughters, became a teacher at a school for the deaf and earned a degree in psychology. Then, in 2003, she was invited to take the same test again and undergo additional testing to determine if she had maintained her girlhood sharpness or was showing signs of cognitive decline. She agreed to do so, but many of her old schoolmates declined, preferring not to have scientists track their mental downswing.

More than 1,000 of McGowan's contemporaries and over 500 from an earlier 1932 survey agreed to participate in the studies that have yielded 250 scientific publications based on 20,000 cognitive tests and brain scans. Most importantly, it offers the first steps toward answering this question: Why do some healthy people maintain their cognitive sharpness as they age, while others lose their edge?

After evaluating the scores on dozens of tests, genetic studies, brain scans, and documentation of lifestyles and health, one factor was found to predict late-life cognitive ability better than any other single measure. It's not exercise, education or any other virtuous activity, but simply the individual's level of intelligence at age 11. Put another way, the more you have in the tank to start, the longer it will last, something that neurophysiologists call the "water tank effect." It matches the concept of cognitive reserve described earlier in these letters.

In fact, the test scores at age 11 account for 50 percent of the variance in IQ at age 77. That leaves half of the variance unaccounted for. In this large cohort, the perceived benefit of healthy things such as alcohol in moderation, and social and intellectual activity seemed to play no role.

People who did not smoke, were physically fit, bilingual or had more education enjoyed slightly higher cognitive test scores than their early life scores would predict. It is likely that genetic and environmental factors also play a role.

Although we tend to think of cognitive decline as a loss of "gray matter" (the brain cells involved with memory and thinking), roughly 10 percent of the variation in late-life IQ scores depends on the integrity of the nerve cell connections. These connections are based on nerve cells that are coated with myelin, which is "white matter." Blotches of white matter show up on testing as "hyperintensities," which signal damage to blood vessels, surrounding cells and the connections between neurons. The cause of these is not well defined, but it may be related to high levels of cortisol, a hormone released in response to stress.

The flip side of cognitive decline with brain aging is an emerging topic with interesting positive aspects.[53] To start with, there are two types of cognitive abilities: "crystallized," such as vocabulary, and "fluid" abilities, which are less dependent on acquired knowledge, such as reasoning and working memory. As a general statement, the age which cognitive skills reach their peak reflects a balance between the time when knowledge accumulation peaks and deterioration of the supporting neural infrastructure begins. There is a lot of truth to the description of people who are older but wiser, for example.

The responses of the brain to aging and shrinkage of the brain itself involve changes in neurotransmitters, flexibility of brain function and neuroplasticity, the latter of which includes actual changes in the brain itself. An example of flexibility of brain function is the ability of the older brain to recruit larger brain areas to respond to tasks. For example, young adults might just use the left frontal cortex to handle large amounts of verbal information in working memory, but older adults will recruit both hemispheres for verbal problems and tasks such as remembering a map.

One mechanism for plasticity is neurogenesis, the growth of new neurons. A number of factors modify plasticity with age. Scientists are now employing two new techniques to study cognition. One involves repetitive magnetic stimulation across specific brain regions to activate or inhibit neural activity. The other uses a battery to administer a small current of electrical energy through two electrodes attached to the scalp. The response of neurostimulation varies with aging. For example, older adults with higher levels of education benefitted from electrical stimulation during a working memory task, whereas those with lower levels of education did not.

This neurostimulation is an influence on brain plasticity that is entirely external. However, there are reasons to believe that emotional, social and motivational situations represent endogenous influences that could affect brain structure and function. For emotion, there is mixed evidence for whether specialized brain regions, such as the amygdala, atrophy more or less than other regions with age. As with cognition, there is a shift to more frontal, rather than posterior, brain regions with age.

Compared to young adults, older adults prefer positive over negative information, perhaps reflecting a motivation to feel good in the time remaining in life. Personality also reflects brain development across the life span. Higher levels of conscientiousness are associated with positive outcomes (larger brain volumes, less volumetric decline), whereas higher levels of neuroticism are associated with poorer outcomes. Education, occupation, leisure activities and high-quality social interactions offer protective effects. With economic tasks, age-related impairments may be greater for losses than gains, which is consistent with the reduced emphasis on negative emotions.

The information presented here comes from a special issue in *Science* devoted to the topic of the aging brain. This is a time of accelerating interest and scientific discovery about the brain. Let's hope that all of us can benefit. We really can't complain about our genetic risk, with Maggie, 96, and Dad now 94 years old.

— Felix

DECEMBER 19, 2014

Dear Family,

This letter started out as another attempt to borrow from the "found objects" school of art. It turns out that the term originates from the French "objet trouvé," describing art created from objects that are not normally considered art, often because they already have a non-art function. They are often presented without commentary. After my visit with the folks yesterday, I tried to be as open as possible to small events. My found objects are lines from two of today's morning readings.

It gets dark so early in the afternoon at this time of year that it's a challenge to visit my parents and make it home while it is still light. That made yesterday an unusual afternoon in itself. I arrived after 3 p.m., and both parents looked lethargic. We got Dad a cup of coffee (which was probably decaffeinated due to his sleeping problem), and I sat with Maggie on her bed, midway between them. The conversations resemble a solitary gymnastic workout. It's not like other circumstances where you can get a conversation going and have others carry the ball for a while. Maggie doesn't speak at all, and Dad is so hard of hearing that the talk has to be very deliberate. His cognitive decline also limits the range of topics, but sometimes there are surprises.

When I sat down on the bed with Maggie, she was obviously glad to see me and stretched out her hand. I held her hand for the rest of the visit, and she kept her gaze on me the entire time. I talked to her and Dad equally, telling them about my day, the trip Caroline and I took to Chicago last weekend, and about my grandkids. Dad asked about the family, and I told him about the situation at work.

Then he looked over at Maggie as she lay with her eyes silently fixed on me. Her face seemed to have a firm expression of interest and concern. He said, "I really think we should take a trip with Sheila (Maggie). She would enjoy it so much." I asked if he had an ocean cruise in mind, and he did. I suggested we would need to take a careful look to identify a cruise line that would be willing to take a passenger who has been confined to bed for 18 months.

Trying to change the subject, I told him about the expanded shipping terminals at Fort Lauderdale that I had heard about. He added that Hilda Haines, the travel agent who arranged our trip around the world 53 years ago, had retired, and no one had come forward to take her place. He has always been one to have loyalty to the people with whom he has worked before. He has asked my sister Sheila if she would be interested in planning the trip, but she was not.

I said it would be OK to take some time to look into such a trip, since there would be sense in waiting until the weather warmed up, so Maggie could make the trip to Florida. Dad said he was very grateful that I was with him in wanting to plan the trip.

The idea of a trip has come up several times over the last few months. It's entirely impractical, of course, but the option of rejecting it doesn't seem appropriate. Dad appears to get genuine pleasure out of planning it, and it's a good opportunity for him to express his love and concern for Maggie. When we took our trip in 1961, he said he planned it as a chance for Maggie to get the extended rest that she really needed. Since then my siblings and I have wondered if Maggie was having a nervous breakdown or if she was just exhausted. Today we might wonder if she had chronic fatigue, depression or a similar malady. I think there is a glimmer of hope for Dad that another ocean journey could have a restorative effect on Maggie's current condition.

This morning, I started with "Song of the Builders," a poem from Mary Oliver's collection, "Why I Wake Early."[54]

"On a summer morning
I sat down
on a hillside
to think about God —

a worthy pastime.
Near me, I saw
a single cricket;
it was moving the grains of sand of the hillside

this way and that way.
How great was its energy,
how humble its effort.
Let us hope

it will always be like this,
each of us going on
in our inexplicable ways
building the universe."

My second reading was from "Silence and Stillness in Every Season" by John Main,[55] a Benedictine monk who died in 1982. His writing for today addresses the topic of the mantra that a meditator uses. He says it is a key to a deeper personal harmony and freedom, but also beyond, to the communion we share with all men and women. The mantra, he asserts, is "an act of pure love, universal love."

He concludes that, "All that we can say in the end is what we said at the beginning — that the meaning of life is the mystery of love."

— Felix

JANUARY 20, 2015

Dear Family,

As Maggie's relentless decline has continued, she makes fewer and fewer gestures. This may be why I'm more impressed with how purposeful her remaining actions are. She is nearly nonverbal, she is completely confined to bed, and I haven't seen her move her legs in months. She can't feed herself. However, when I approach the bedside, she fixes her gaze on me and usually holds out a hand for me to grasp. Sometimes she points. Her facial expression seems to indicate that she recognizes me.

Last Thursday, I was getting ready to leave when I heard her speak. I turned on my heel and came back to the bedside. Her caregiver, Nela, was sitting on the bed, getting ready to offer her a smoothie, her usual late afternoon snack.

"Did Maggie just talk? What did she say?" I asked Nela.

Nela answered that Maggie had just said one word, "Worry." That's what I had thought I heard, too. Now, why would she say that? Was it completely random, or was there a reason for her to say "worry"?

We remained quietly at her bedside for a few minutes, trying to coax another word from her. She didn't speak, but it was then that we both noticed a deep, rasping cough.

The next day the cough was more frequent, so I phoned in a prescription for a broad-spectrum antibiotic. Over the weekend, there was no significant change.

On Monday, she was clearly worse, and Sheila and the caregivers were concerned. I switched her to the powerful antibiotic that she had taken for the episode of pneumonia in September and said I would stop by after work. At first glance, she seemed better in the afternoon, but I noticed her breathing rate was increased at 26 breaths per minute (normal is 14-16).

Today, Maggie was noticeably worse in the morning. Sheila woke Dad, so he could be with her. Jody and I juggled our schedules, so we could be there at midday, and the hospice nurse was summoned. Her respiratory rate was up to 30 breaths per minute, and Maggie had a rattle in her throat. Her face was blank. Her eyes were fixed straight ahead. She didn't blink at all, and she was unresponsive to our presence. The hospice nurse was so sweet. She checked Maggie professionally, and then started her on some tablets of atropine, a form of belladonna, to dry up the secretions that were causing her throat to rattle.

This evening, Maggie seemed to have aged more in the six hours since I'd seen her last than she had in the last six weeks. Her breathing rate was up to 36, and her mouth was now wide open. The strongest predictor of mortality in patients with pneumonia is the breathing rate.

Dad has been at Maggie's side since he had been wakened at 11 this morning. He has slept for much of the time, which we attribute to the emotional strain of Maggie's condition. He's asked if Maggie might have had a small stroke to account for why she is not responding to us. He keeps asking if there is anything else we should be doing for her. Sheila has been so helpful, gently reassuring him that the doctors have done everything that they could, and we just have to let Maggie sleep, in case she might be better in the morning. She led us in congratulating him on his love and skillful management of Maggie's health issues, which have allowed her to live this long.

Jody, Sheila and I sat in chairs and on the bed on Maggie's right side, next to Dad. Nela and Mira, the caregivers, sat on the floor on Maggie's left side, looking a little bit as if they were at a slumber party because of their young age. It's been a tough week worldwide, with terrorist attacks and suicide bombers, but there was so much love and kindness in the room as we gathered with Maggie for what we all feel to be the last time.

— Felix

JANUARY 31, 2015

Dear Family,

We held a grand and poignant funeral for Maggie on Sunday.

She died a few minutes after 1 a.m. on January 21.

Sheila and the two caregivers, Nela and Mira, were with her. They got Dad up about 2:30 a.m. He sat with Maggie until dawn. Jody came over then, and so did the police and the hospice nurse. Martenson's Funeral Home representatives arrived to pick Maggie up about 8:30 a.m. Dad asked Jody if he would listen to her lungs one more time, just to check if Maggie might still be breathing.

Dad usually sleeps until noon or so, and he often dozes off during the afternoon. This day he was up continuously from the early morning hours, and he grew increasingly more restless and agitated. Throughout the day, at least two people were with him at all times, and he asked the same questions over and over. He wanted reassurances that Maggie was all right and that she was being watched carefully at Martenson's. Even two days later, he wanted to know if they had someone watching over her, so that they would notice if she took a breath. We had to reassure him that was the case, even though she had been cremated by then. Later we agreed that the "official" time of the cremation was Sunday afternoon.

I've read reports of Buddhist masters that enter a gradual death spiral and very slowly wither away until the bodily remains and the soul seem to depart at the same time. Maggie was a bit like that. It's hard to know, but she may have dwindled to about 70 pounds. She had virtually no material possessions — a few nightgowns and pajamas, a nearby dresser, a rented hospital bed and a few boxes of diapers. Despite all of this, and knowing for a long time that this day was inevitable, we suddenly had a lot of things to do. We needed to prepare an obituary announcement for the papers, notify a few close friends and start arrangements for the funeral service itself.

Between us four siblings, we had four versions of how to put together a service. We agreed on two important ground rules: The goal was to develop a service that would be what Maggie would have wanted, and we each tacitly agreed to let go of our viewpoint when confronted with a different view from one of us or the minister. Somehow, all of us contributed to the obituary notice, and it still read pretty smoothly. We all had a hand in the design of the service, and the program got printed on time.

The service was held at St. James on Grosse Ile, the church home for our parents beginning about 1950. We originally planned the service for the small chapel, since we just anticipated our family and a few friends. The chapel was built in the late 1860s and seats about 75 people. We were advised that would not accommodate the number of people likely to attend. The service was moved to the new church, which isn't nearly as intimate or comforting, but at least Dad had been on the building committee that helped to arrange its construction.

We all sat down front, and Dad was in a large chair placed for him in the row reserved for wheelchairs. The service began with a bagpipe procession. Have you ever heard the strange sounds that a bagpipe makes in the few seconds before the notes come forth? It's a haunting, strange hiss. Then the loud honking music.

The rector invited us to consider the service in terms of Easter, since the funeral finds its meaning in the resurrection. There were three eulogies, one by our sister Lisa, and the other two given by our childhood neighbors, Valerie Overholt and Jim Deering. All speakers are at risk for crying, if not blubbering, at funerals, but these three speakers were each endearing, steadfast and moving. The readings were by my daughters, Elizabeth and Alison, and Jody's son, Toby. After the service, the bagpiper led us into the parish hall for lunch. Jody and I had brought enough wine for an army, and it served us well. Since, in this case, no one could bear a grudge for an untimely death, there was a mood of celebration in the room. Maggie's was indeed a life well lived.

— Felix

Epilogue

I'VE FOUND MYSELF APPROACHING THIS FINAL LETTER over and over. Just as it is hard to let Maggie go, this way of getting in touch with my feelings has become an important part of my interior life, one that I don't want to relinquish. I know that I have made a generous compliment to myself by classifying myself as a "writer" with these letters, but the writing of them has been an enriching experience.

The reader might be surprised to learn of our immediate response to Maggie's death.

My brother and I just went off to work. I arrived on time to see morning office patients. Jody stopped by the condo to meet the police and representatives from the funeral home, and he arrived 30 minutes late for office hours. Maggie died early on a Friday, so Lisa finished her morning patients at the office in Cleveland and left that afternoon for Grosse Ile. Sheila spent the day with Dad. Jody and I were able to get to the condo in the early afternoon, as our cardiology partner and physician assistants agreed to cover our hospital patients.

This is one of the strange ways of physicians. Our sense of mission and duty is so strong that I think the typical doctor who broke his leg on his way to work would just stop in the Orthopedics Department once he arrived to get some crutches to see him through until he could get the leg X-rayed in his spare time. There are a lot more women in medicine today, but I don't think it has changed this behavior pattern.

The other aspect is that Maggie's decline and eventual death had taken so much of our physical and emotional energy that we had been running on empty for several months prior to her death. Each of us formed a strategy to cope with the demands of the situation and to move ahead with business as usual, as best we could. In addition to this stress, both of

Caroline's parents had health issues that were like bookends to my parents' situation. Her father died of dementia the year before Maggie died, and her mother died nine months after our Dad had succumbed.

Maggie and Dad outlived just about all their friends. With social media and email, it didn't take us long to notify family members, professional associates, and the few friends and neighbors who had kept in touch.

These letters describe the time-consuming and expensive aspects of providing care for invalid parents. After Maggie died, one of our first challenges was to make new arrangements with the caregivers. Although it might seem at first that the expense would decrease, we still needed 24-hour care, and Dad's needs were much more intensive than Maggie's since she had been completely bedridden. He needed help with ambulation and all of his meals blended to go in his feeding tube. Sheila handled the negotiations with the caregivers. First, we provided them substantial tips for their loving care to our mom. Then she discussed the new pay scale. It hardly differed from the previous one.

As a family, we four kids took a hard look at Dad's financial reserves. He had social security, a tiny pension of $600 a month and a small amount of cash remaining from the sale of his house in Florida. With the current housing arrangements, the salaries of the caregivers, food and other expenses, we calculated that we had six months of reserve funds. After that, we knew each of us would need to contribute, beginning in July.

Dad was deeply depressed for weeks after Maggie's death. Even though she hadn't walked in two years and was bedridden for 18 months, he had never really acknowledged her decline and its inevitable end. We tried to be with him as much as we could. Perhaps the biggest problem was the disruption in his sleep cycle. He would try to go to bed by midnight, but he was typically up all night. He would ring for the caregivers to take him to the bathroom throughout the night, sometimes several times in an hour. He then would sleep throughout the entire day. He would often be asleep when we came to visit. We consulted several of our colleagues with expertise in gerontology, but nothing we tried helped. The caregivers did their best to take turns sleeping, but they were rapidly becoming exhausted.

∞ ∞ ∞ ∞ ∞ ∞ ∞ ∞ ∞ ∞ ∞ ∞ ∞ ∞ ∞

Below is an excerpt from an email I sent to my family in early May 2015. It captures some of the issues we were dealing with:

Dear Family,

I want to give you an update on my father's status. I'll start with two anecdotes from earlier this week:

On May 6, I got over to Dad's place and said hello. With some urgency, he replied, "I need to have your telephone number in case we need you right away." One of the caregivers, Mira, went scrambling and returned with a master list of all the phone numbers for everybody in the family. Dad set the list down on the end table and went on to say that he had seen some hummingbirds at the feeder that I had put up two days before!

Then Luda, the other caregiver from the Ukraine, told me earlier that day she had seen a man find a large "tortilla." She held her arms in a circle in front of her. (This close to Cinco de Mayo, I pictured something for the largest taco in town.) When she said the man then put it in the pond in front of the condo, I realized what she was talking about. We said all this in voices loud enough for Dad to hear, and he replied, "I've seen two turtles that big in my life, and I ate both of them."

Dad can spend a few hours in coherent conversation and even express his sense of humor. He's talked poignantly with Sheila and Lisa about being a dad, some of his regrets about parenting and how much he misses Maggie. He can also spend hours at a time deeply asleep. When I visited Friday, he had been sleeping all day and didn't wake the entire time I was there. I left at 5:30 without exchanging a single word with him. Dad is winding down and doing so with the inconsistency that the hospice literature predicts, with waxing and waning degrees of withdrawal and quiet. He's also taken up an interest in the television that he's never had before. A few weeks ago, he watched the Detroit Red Wings in their short-lived run in the Stanley Cup hockey playoffs, and now he's catching up on Detroit Tigers baseball. The caregivers entice him into a few TV shows, and now and again, he'll watch an old-time western or romantic drama. Nonetheless, he's maintained the calm and inscrutable demeanor that all of us recall from our childhood. It's hard to draw the line between his efforts to remain in control and a quiet acceptance of the inevitable.

We couldn't ask for more sweet and caring help than Mira and Luda provide. They are charming and devoted to Dad. We four kids do our best to get over there and visit. Sheila has taken the lead in supervising his care, for which the rest of us are so grateful.

— Felix

∞ ∞ ∞ ∞ ∞ ∞ ∞ ∞ ∞ ∞ ∞ ∞ ∞ ∞ ∞ ∞

As the six-month time frame approached, we were discouraged to find out that our calculations were exactly right: We were just about out of money. We tried as many creative approaches as we could imagine. The folks had bought a 650-acre farm in West Virginia in 1976, and then, when they moved to Arizona, they sold all but 10 acres, which included the mouth to the Norman Cave, one of the 10 largest caves in North America.

Although it had been deeded to us four children, we tried to sell it. Not only were there no comparable properties in the area to help us set the price tag, but the local real estate agents also told us not to bother because nothing was selling in that county. We considered renting out the lower floor of the condo, since it was unused, but decided it was too impractical, even for the target buyer of a medical student needing a place to stay for a month or two. We looked into other types of care settings, including adult foster care, a smaller apartment or even a nursing home. In the end, we kept him in his condo, looking out on a small pond, just a half-mile from our childhood home.

We all felt Dad's last weeks and months were tragically uncomfortable. He found the feeding tube very annoying. In the fall, another small brainstem stroke seriously impaired his speech function. He lapsed into a coma several days before he died. His breathing pattern was regular and deep, with the characteristic "death rattle" from thick oral secretions. A day or two before he died, we noticed a remarkable change in his circulatory system. By this time, he hadn't had any food in a couple of days, and he was undoubtedly seriously dehydrated. His body somehow realigned his circulatory system into a survival mode. We could not get a blood pressure reading, and none of his pulses were palpable. We assumed he was shunting all of his blood supply to his brain and diverting it from the peripheral tissues in his arms and legs. Only a stubborn, highly determined cardiologist would have such a response.

He died in the early morning hours of December 11.

Dad's funeral service was poignant and understated. And it proved deeply moving for many people. Because of his background with brass music throughout high school and college, we enlisted a superb trumpet player, who accompanied the hymns and offered Aaron Copland's "Quiet City" as a meditation. The Rev. Phil Dinwidddy was right on target with his homily. No one else has gotten our dad so right as he did that day, recognizing him as someone who was able to see things the rest of us did not perceive and who was sufficiently skilled to bring his vision to fruition.

His obituary extolled him as a pioneer in osteopathic medicine, and cited his leadership in cardiology and internal medicine. He had many interests outside the world of medicine and established a program for the certification of organic food in the early 1980s. He loved gardening and beekeeping. He was as active as Maggie in St. James Church, where he sang in the choir, served on its vestry and oversaw the environmental committee. My father's greatest legacy may have been to instill a sense of responsibility to serve others, whether through medicine or other humanitarian means.

One interesting expression of condolence came from Bill Redding, a classmate and perhaps the only graduate of our high school who would go on to play college football in a Rose Bowl Game. Bill remembered my father's connection with the world of amateur and professional wrestling.

Dad did the cardiac evaluation on the most famous of the local professional wrestlers, including Leaping Larry Chene, Haystack Calhoun and Happy Humphrey. However, I don't think he ever took care of the most famous, Dick the Bruiser. I remember Dad saying that one wrestler was so heavy they couldn't get him up on an exam table to do his EKG as it wouldn't hold him. They asked him to lie on the floor. Once there, he was so out of shape, he couldn't get back up without assistance. The wrestler commented that if any opponent got him to the mat, the match was over, since he would never be able to get up. I recall that my dad advised him to quit the sport and lose weight. He died a few years after that evaluation.

About that time, Dad served as the physician for the Greco-Roman World Wrestling Championship, which was held in Toledo, Ohio. While Jody and I went down for one of the matches, our dad attended all of them. I remember that Dad had wrestled while in high school, but I don't recall any specific training in sports medicine. Good thing no one was hurt.

Notes and letters trickled in from friends and professional colleagues. I became convinced that there is no statute of limitations on a letter of condolence. It is never too late. This excerpt from an email sent by another high school classmate Tom Woodward was a source of great comfort:

"People will miss both your father and your mother. I am saddened by their passing but happy that they enjoyed the long, loving and productive lives that they both so graciously lived. I always found them to be warm, welcoming and humble. The world will miss them. I miss them."

Over the ensuing years, I have missed them both and discovered the rich variety of circumstances when they come to mind. Sometimes the associations are obvious, as when I drive by our childhood home, or when we recall traditional family gatherings such as Thanksgiving or Mother's Day. More often, I'm caught by surprise and find myself saying something like, "Hmmm, what made me think of Maggie just now?" Exploring that event often calls forth strong recollections and deep emotions. Whenever possible, if I hear that call, I try to follow that trail of feelings.

It may be analogous to the statement by Kahlil Gibran quoted earlier in these Maggie Letters, as he urges us:

"When love beckons, follow him."

In this case, it occurs as a gentle reminder that love does survive death.

My parents live on in another way. Things of their lives have been incorporated in to my own life, either as thought patterns, facial expressions or physical mannerisms. A hot topic in science nowadays is epigenetics, the manifestation of physical or behavioral events due to changes in gene expression, that can't be accounted for directly on the basis of the genetic code. I don't know enough about that topic to test its relevance to this idea, but I do find myself acting out gestures that I recall from my father or making up jokes in the style of my mother. Since my parents' illness sensitized me to the need for brain health, bone health and hearing health, I try to take advantage of every chance I get to work on these things, much as my father did with practicing yoga for the eyes.

Recently, when I was walking with my wife, I stepped up onto the curb, to practice my balance as we walked along. I told her that balance training is a teachable skill. Her first reply was to let me know it looked like I was "walking like a dork." Then she shrugged her shoulders and said, "You are your father's son."

I'd like to offer yet one more observation on the impact of a memory or emotion: I am occasionally caught by a sudden pang. An idea or a person may come to mind, and I can't complete the thought or round out the details of the person. Instinctively, I want to turn to my parents to fill in the blanks. I am disappointed anew that they are not here.

Maggie was proud of what she called her "junk mind," the ability to carry all manner of arcane facts and personal information. With Mom and

Dad passing, our information source is gone, too. Each of us kids have moved up in line, and now we are the senior guardians of the family heritage. It makes me want to organize every important piece of family information that I can, to finish the genealogy project as soon as I get this off my desk and document the new events as our family continues to grow.

Sifting through boxes of photos, letters and news clippings, I came across a scrap of paper with Maggie's distinctive handwriting. On it was a quote that she recited to us many times. She attributed it to Henry van Dyke, but it is actually by the British Quaker, Harold Loukes (1912-1980). That small error in attribution does not detract from its appropriateness here since it is a consolation for me as I end this project, still nagged with uncertainty about the value these Maggie Letters will have for my family and a readership at large:

> *A gift of love that fails is as much a part of the divine life as a gift that succeeds because love is measured by its fullness and not by its reception.*

— Felix

Notes

1. The condition now known as Alzheimer's disease was first described by Alois Alzheimer on November 3, 1906. He reported the unusual case of Auguste Deter to the Society of Southwest German Psychiatrists. Her symptoms included delusional jealousy, paranoia and memory loss, which began gradually at the age of 51, and progressed until she died at age 55. After her death on April 8, 1906, Alzheimer identified in her brain amyloid plaques, neurofibrillary tangles and arteriosclerotic changes. These continue to be the salient pathological findings of the disease.

This case presentation led to the original idea that Alzheimer's disease was a rare cause of pre-senile dementia. It wasn't until the mid-1970s that the disease was reported to be the cause of senile dementia in the elderly. From its initial consideration as a rare condition, Alzheimer's disease then came to be understood as highly prevalent, a major cause of dementia at any age and a major cause of death. (This historical vignette is described more completely in an excellent review paper on Alzheimer's disease for clinicians by Richard J. Caselli and colleagues at the Mayo Clinic, Mayo Clinic Proceedings, June 2017: 92(6):978-994.)

My mother referred to my grandmother's condition as "senility," which, ironically, was a synonym for pre-senile dementia. Both terms have fallen out of favor. Modern medical terminology now favors the naming of medical conditions with a person's name alone, not as a possessive. So, the preferred term is Alzheimer disease. However, since the expected audience for this book is the lay public, I have retained the older, and more widely used form, Alzheimer's disease.

These letters began in 2009, and medical research has advanced rapidly since that time. As a general statement, I have tried to avoid presenting detailed scientific information or treatment advice, in large part because of the likelihood that today's best ideas may end up on tomorrow's scrapheap. In preparing this manuscript for publication, I took every effort to be sure that the facts presented here were consistent with our most current information on Alzheimer's disease. I've tried to stay current with the literature on Alzheimer's, and the text has been updated as appropriate.

2. Meyer Friedman (July 13, 1910 – April 27, 2001). Personal communication to my brother, Joseph C. Rogers, DO, 1984.

3. Henry van Dyke. "Foot-Path to Peace." This poem was published in the Tacoma Times on January 1, 1904.

4. "A Child's Christmas in Wales." This is the recording we listened to each year just before the Christmas holiday break: https://www.youtube.com/watch?v=Hv4-sgFw3Go
Published on July 20, 2013. Digitized from the LP shown above, "Dylan Thomas Reading Volume 1," issued on the Caedmon label in 1964, catalogue number TC 1002. Recorded February 22, 1952, at Steinway Hall in New York.

5. "Do Not Go Gentle Into That Good Night." This poem was written as an homage to Dylan Thomas' father after his death. When Thomas died, Igor Stravinsky set these words to music in tribute to the poet. The work is scored for tenor, strings and four trombones.

6. We joked about the frequency with which salmon appeared on the menu, and I just assumed that it represented my father's limited skill set after a lifetime of avoiding any domestic duties until he was forced to start cooking. In 2016, the medical literature was full of reports that demonstrated the Mediterranean diet, and fish in particular, was effective in preventing or delaying the onset of Alzheimer's disease. Here's one example:
Huhn S, Masouleh SH, Stumvoll M, Villringer A and Witte AV. "Components of a Mediterranean diet and their impact on cognitive functions in aging." Frontiers in Aging Neuroscience, www.frontiersin.org, 1 July 2015, Volume 7, Article 132.

7. Leo Tolstoy. The Three Hermits (1886), from "The Raid and Other Stories," translated by Louise and Aylmer Maude, Oxford University Press, 1982. New York. pp. 280-288.

8. Published online on July 20, 2017, by Livingston G, Sommerlad A, Orgeta V, et al. in *The Lancet*, http://www.thelancet.com/pdfs/journals/lancet/PIIS0140-6736(17)31363-6.pdf.

9. "Jesus and the Fig Tree." This story appears in two places in the Gospels: Matthew 21: 18-22 and Mark 11: 12-14, 20-25. See commentary in Mary Gordon, "Reading Jesus. A Writer's Encounter with the Gospels." Pantheon Books, New York. 2009, pp. 56-62.

10. "Rejoice always, pray without ceasing, give thanks in all circumstances." 1 Thessalonians 5: 16-18. New Revised Standard Version.

11. J. D. Salinger. "Franny and Zooey." Little, Brown. 1961.

12. John Main. "Silence and Stillness in Every Season." The Continuum Publishing Company. New York, New York. 1997. Daily reading for November 25.

13. Dean Ornish, MD. "Dr. Dean Ornish's Program for Reversing Heart Disease." Random House. 1990.

14. Gina Kolata. "Insights Give Hope for New Attack on Alzheimer's." *New York Times*, December 13, 2010. http://www.nytimes.com/2010/12/14/health/14alzheimers.html?pagewanted=all

15. Mawuenyega KG, Sigurdson W, Ovod V, et al. Decreased clearance of CNS B-amyloid in Alzheimer's disease. *Science* December 24, 2010, 330: 1774. www.sciencemag.org

16. His Holiness The Dalai Lama. Calm Abiding, in "An Open Heart. Practicing Compassion in Everyday Life." Little, Brown and Company, Boston, New York, London. 2001. Chapter 11, p. 129-137.

17. Mason MF, Norton MI, Van Horn JD, Wegner DM, Grafton ST, and Macrae CN. "Wandering Minds: The Default Network and Stimulus-Independent Thought," www.sciencemag.org Science Vol. 315, 19 January 2007, pp. 393-395. Doi 10.1126/science.1131295.

18. Oliver Sacks. "This year, change your mind." *New York Times*, December 31, 2010.
http://www.nytimes.com/2011/01/01/opinion/01sacks.html

19. Pam Belluck, "Giving Alzheimer patients their way, even chocolate." *New York Times*, December 31, 2010.
http://www.nytimes.com/2011/01/01/health/01care.html?ref=health

20. Loose associations in the speech of persons with Alzheimer's disease. The authors of "A Caregiver's Guide to Alzheimer's Disease," offer tips for making life easier. They use the ploy of lunch in a restaurant to show the progression of loss in memory, language and social tasks as the cognitive decline worsens.
Callone PR, Kudlacek C, Vasiloff BC, Manternach J and Brumback RA. "A Caregiver's Guide to Alzheimer's Disease. 300 tips for making life easier." Demos Medical Publishing, LLC, New York. 2006.

21. Out of an entire shelf of books about Alzheimer's disease, I chose these two, almost at random. They proved to be of great value.
Callone PR, Kudlacek C, Vasiloff BC, Manternach J and Brumback RA. "A Caregiver's Guide to Alzheimer's Disease. 300 tips for making life easier." Demos Medical Publishing, LLC, New York. 2006.
Joanne Koenig Coste. "Learning to speak Alzheimer's. A groundbreaking approach for everyone dealing with the disease." A Mariner Book, Houghton Mifflin Company, Boston and New York. 2003.

22. James, W. "Principles of Psychology (Vol. 1)," New York: Henry-Holt and Co. 1890. Quoted in Farb, et al, which follows.
Farb NAS, Segal ZV, Mayberg H, et al. Attending to the present: mindfulness meditation reveals distinct neural modes of self-reference. *SCAN* 2007; 2: 313-322.

23. J. Krishnamurti. "The Book of Life. Daily Meditations with Krishnamurti." Daily meditation for January 28. HarperOne, an imprint of HarperCollinsPublishers. New York. 1995.

24. Joanne Koenig Coste. "Learning to speak Alzheimer's. A groundbreaking approach for everyone dealing with the disease." A Mariner Book, Houghton Mifflin Company, Boston and New York. 2003.

25. The "Prayer of St. Patrick" as typically recited is actually a section of a longer prayer, more properly called "St. Patrick's Breastplate." Here's how the website, "Our Catholic Prayers," (http://www.ourcatholicprayers.com/st-patricks-breastplate.html) describes it:

"St. Patrick's Breastplate is a popular prayer attributed to one of Ireland's most beloved patron saints. According to tradition, St. Patrick wrote it in 433 A.D. for divine protection before successfully converting the Irish King Leoghaire and his subjects from paganism to Christianity. (The term breastplate refers to a piece of armor worn in battle.)"

The description of the prayer adds this sidebar to the idea of a breastplate:

"When St. Paul referred to putting on the 'Armor of God' in his letter to the Ephesians (6:11) to fight sin and evil inclinations, he could have been thinking of prayers just like this one! We may not wear combat gear in our daily lives, but St. Patrick's Breastplate can function as divine armor for protection against spiritual adversity."

26. These risk factors for Alzheimer's disease have stood the test of time, at least in the short term. At the Alzheimer's Association International Conference held in London on July 20, 2017, data were presented from the Lancet Commission on dementia prevention, intervention and care. They reported that 35 percent of cases of Alzheimer's are preventable. They detailed the following nine contributing conditions and the relative role of each in causing the disease:

Nine factors that contribute to the risk of dementia:
Midlife hearing loss – responsible for 9 percent of the risk
Failing to complete secondary education – 8 percent
Smoking – 5 percent
Failing to seek early treatment for depression – 4 percent

Physical inactivity – 3 percent

Social isolation – 2 percent

High blood pressure – 2 percent

Obesity – 1 percent

Type 2 diabetes – 1 percent

These risk factors—which are described as potentially modifiable—
add up to 35 percent. The other 65 percent of dementia risk is thought to
be potentially non-modifiable.

http://www.thelancet.com/pdfs/journals/lancet/PIIS0140-
6736(17)31363-6.pdf

27. David Eagleman. "Incognito. The secret lives of the brain." Pantheon
Books, New York. 2011. Chapter 4. "The kinds of thoughts that are
thinkable." pp. 75-100.

28. Mary Beckman. February 17, 2003, "12 a.m. Alien Abduction.
Memories of Space." Science www.sciencemag.org/news/2003/.../
memories-space-alien-abduction.

29. Judith Valente and Charles Reynard. "Twenty Poems to Nourish Your
Soul." Loyola Press, Chicago. 2006.

30. https://en.wikipedia.org/wiki/The_Windhover.

31. Marcus E. Raichle. "The Brain's Dark Energy," *Science*, 24 Nov
2006. science.sciencemag.org/content/314/5803/1249 DOI: 10.1126/
science. 1134405. Original figure from: Fox MD, Snyder AZ, Vincent JL,
Corbetta M, Van Essen DC, Raichle ME. The human brain is intrinsically
organized into dynamic, anti-correlated functional networks PNAS
2005 102 (27) 9673-9678; published ahead of print June 23, 2005,
doi:10.1073/pnas.0504136102.

There is another perspective on this idea of the natural coherence
of brain function. Our biologic inheritance is to have a brain that
functions perfectly well on its own. Fortunately, the normative state is
for the majority of the brain to have this well-synchronized function and
contaminating ideas are a small percentage of brain activity. The trick is

in the control of this pesky small fraction. If we don't invoke executive function in response to our present environment, the default brain takes over. We risk the possibility that our wakeful thoughts are turned over to daydreaming. In turn, that places us at risk to allow judgments, the commentary of our "inner roommate," or negative emotions to take over our thoughts.

The smooth-running function of the brain is something all of us have experienced at some time. It happens when an athlete gets "in the zone." Mihaly Csikszentmihalyi, the emeritus professor of psychology at the University of Chicago, described it as "flow" in his book of the same name.

If we can omit or control the constant barrage of thoughts that sway our lives, we attain the state the Buddhists call "no-ideas," which can also be translated as emptiness. This full, uncontaminated state is the Buddha nature. In mystical Christianity, it is prayer that represents contact with the (unceasing) stream of love that flows between Jesus and the Father. In ordinary, everyday terms, this is mindfulness.

32. Sri Ramakrishna, Bengal, 1836-1886. Quoted in John Main, "Silence and Stillness in Every Season," daily reading for September 28.

33. Interview with Michael Gazzaniga on how the split-brain experiments unlocked our understanding of the need to tell stories, of how the right brain is "the interpreter." Includes an interview with Gazzaniga:
Benedict Carey. "Decoding the Brain's Cacophony," Profiles in Science, *New York Times*, October 31, 2011. The following year, this reference provides additional background:
Wolman D. "A tale of two halves." Nature. 483: 2012. pp. 260-263.
This classic article is now seen as the reference that established the new way of seeing brain function: Gazzaniga MS. "Organization of the human brain." *Science* 245: 1989. pp. 947–952.

34. "The Essential Henri Nouwen," edited by Robert A. Jonas. Shambala Press, Boston and London. 2009. Chapter 5, "Sacred Mourning," pp. 58-76.

35. Isaiah 64:1-9.

"O that you would tear open the heavens and come down, so that the mountains would quake at your presence — [2]as when fire kindles brushwood and the fire causes water to boil — to make your name known to your adversaries, so that the nations might tremble at your presence! [3]When you did awesome deeds that we did not expect, you came down, the mountains quaked at your presence. [4]From ages past no one has heard, no ear has perceived, no eye has seen any God besides you, who works for those who wait for him. [5]You meet those who gladly do right, those who remember you in your ways. But you were angry, and we sinned; because you hid yourself we transgressed.

[6]We have all become like one who is unclean, and all our righteous deeds are like a filthy cloth. We all fade like a leaf, and our iniquities, like the wind, take us away. [7]There is no one who calls on your name, or attempts to take hold of you; for you have hidden your face from us, and have delivered us into the hand of our iniquity. [8]Yet, O Lord, you are our Father; we are the clay, and you are our potter; we are all the work of your hand. [9]Do not be exceedingly angry, O Lord, and do not remember iniquity forever. Now consider, we are all your people.

36. 1 Corinthians 1:3-9 New Revised Standard Version (NRSV).

3) Grace to you and peace from God our Father and the Lord Jesus Christ. 4) I give thanks to my God always for you because of the grace of God that has been given you in Christ Jesus, 5) for in every way you have been enriched in him, in speech and knowledge of every kind— 6) just as the testimony of Christ has been strengthened among you — 7) so that you are not lacking in any spiritual gift as you wait for the revealing of our Lord Jesus Christ. 8) He will also strengthen you to the end, so that you may be blameless on the day of our Lord Jesus Christ. 9) God is faithful; by him you were called into the fellowship of his Son, Jesus Christ our Lord.

37. The O Antiphons: https://en.wikipedia.org/wiki/O_Antiphons

38. Kahlil Gibran. "The Prophet." Alfred A. Knopf, New York. 1965. pp. 11-14.

39. For more on our "Cousin Willie," the Bishop of Sialkot, Pakistan, 1970-1977, see William G. Young, "Presbyterian Bishop." New Millenium, London. 1995. ISBN 1 85845 039 X.

40. P.D. Ouspensky. "The Fourth Way. A Record of Talks and Answers to Questions Based on the Teachings of G.I. Gurdjieff." Alfred A. Knopf, New York. 1965.

41. Anonymous, "Meditations on the Tarot. A Journey into Christian Hermeticism." Letter XIII, "Death." Jeremy P. Tarcher/Putnam, New York. 1985. p. 354-361 (This section includes long quotations from P.D. Ouspensky, "In Search of the Miraculous." Alfred A. Knopf, London. 1969.)

42. Genesis 3-5. (NRSV):
"**3)** but God said, 'You shall not eat of the fruit of the tree that is in the middle of the garden, nor shall you touch it, or you shall die.' **4)** But the serpent said to the woman, "You will not die, **5)** for God knows that when you eat of it your eyes will be opened, and you will be like God, knowing good and evil."

43. Thich Nhat Hanh. "Peace is Every Step. The Path of Mindfulness in Everyday Life." New York, Bantam. 1991.

44. Thich Nhat Hanh. "Your True Home: Everyday Wisdom of Thich Nhat Hanh." Shambala, Boston & London. 2011.

45. Morell V, et al. "In the minds of birds." *Science* 05 Jul 2013: Vol. 341, Issue 6141, p. 22-25. DOI: 10.1126/science.341.6141.22.

46. Pandharipande PP, Girard TD, Jackson JC, et al. for the BRAIN-ICU Study Investigators. Long-Term Cognitive Impairment after Critical Illness." *New England Journal of Medicine*, 2013; 369:1306-1316 October 3, 2013. DOI: 10.1056/NEJMoa1301372

47. https://www.frick.org/exhibitions/mauritshuis/149, accessed September 24, 2017.

48. John Main. "Silence and Stillness in Every Season." Daily reading for August 31.

49. Jack Kornfield. "A Path With Heart. A Guide Through the Perils and Promises of Spiritual Life." Bantam Books, New York. 1993.

50. Emily Underwood. In-Depth Nobel Prizes, "Brain's GPS Finds Top Honor." *Science* 10 Oct 2014: Vol. 346, Issue 6206, pp. 149. DOI: 10.1126/science.346.6206.149-a.

51. *Science*, "Special Issue: The Aging Brain." 31 Oct 2014.

52. Emily Underwood. "The Aging Brain." Starting young. *Science* 31 Oct 2014: Vol. 346, Issue 6209, pp. 568-571. DOI: 10.1126/science.346.6209.568.

53. Angela Gutchess. "Plasticity of the aging brain: New directions in cognitive neuroscience." *Science* 31 Oct 2014: Vol. 346, Issue 6209,pp. 579-582. DOI: 10.1126/science.1254604.

54. Mary Oliver. "Song of the Builders," from "Why I Wake Early." Beacon Press, Boston. 2004. p. 60.

55. John Main. "Silence and Stillness in Every Season," Reading for December 19.

About the Author

FELIX J. ROGERS, DO is a cardiologist in the Henry Ford Health System and is a clinical professor of internal medicine at Michigan State University College of Osteopathic Medicine. He has been active in medical societies and in organizations working for social change, including Physicians for Social Responsibility. He directed the Cranbrook Peace Foundation for 23 years. He now volunteers for Focus: HOPE in Detroit, joining their efforts to eliminate poverty, racism and injustice. Felix is a member of Christ Church Cranbrook in Bloomfield Hills, Michigan, where he attended a weekly program for meditation and contemplative reading for more than 20 years. He met Caroline Bell while in medical school and married her soon thereafter. They have two daughters, Elizabeth and Alison, and three grandchildren.